awaken into flow

# Advance Praise for *Awaken Into Flow*

"Writing a book will challenge you, to say the least, or free you. Likely both. When you get out of your head and into your heart, you will find the courage and stamina necessary to overcome your hang-ups and finish your book. This lovely book can be your guide."

**ANNE LAMOTT** #1 *New York Times* best-selling author of *Bird by Bird* and *Somehow*

"Having birthed my book with Catherine, I gained so much more than I realized I was investing in. When the work began with a guided meditation and grounding practice, I knew I was in the right place for my soul to be a channel for my writing. To move out of the head and into the heart and to allow the words to flow. Each chakra activation practice allowed me to connect to another depth of inner wisdom while releasing blocks holding me from true alignment. If you're looking to shift out of hustle mode and into your authentic zone of genius in becoming an author, Catherine will be your sage guide."

**MARYBETH HYLAND** Speaker, Coach, and Author of *Permission to Be Human: The Conscious Leader's Guide to Creating a Values-Driven Culture*

"I recently wrote a book using Catherine's FLOW Method, which took me out of my discomfort zone where I was facing impostor syndrome and writer's block. After removing the roadblocks that my ego was setting up and letting the words flow naturally, I wound up with a book I never believed I could write. Catherine's guidance and innate ability to help a first-time author take an idea from concept to finished product is remarkable. I recommend *Awaken Into Flow* to anyone who has a story to share."

**MICHAEL BUSH** Managing Partner of GrowthWays Partners, LLC, and Author of *Guardrailing: Authentically Guide Your Natural Products Company from Spark to Sale*

"The principles that Catherine shares in her new book *Awaken Into Flow* are the main reason I'm now a published author and not just an aspiring one. Catherine's gentle, positive, and consistent guidance helped my business partner and me translate our dreams of 'one day writing a book' into an outline, then a draft, then an edited manuscript, and now a book that has already been purchased by readers in eight different countries. If you're reading this, you already know you want to write a book. That's the first step. Now, invest in your own vision by reading *Awaken Into Flow*. You *can* publish a book—and Catherine can help."

    **JEFF SHUCK**  Principal, Plenty Consulting and Author of *Leading with Light: Choosing Conscious Leadership When You're Ready for More*

"While many books are available on the craft and business of becoming a published author, none will bring this goal to fruition unless the writer is in flow. In *Awaken Into Flow*, Catherine gently leads you, like a trusted friend, from inspiration to the final word by addressing the energy needed to become a published author happy with your finished book. Using her powerful exercises—from chakra breathwork to the Writer Frequency Scale to inviting your fears in for tea—*Awaken Into Flow* will allow you to connect with the voice and wisdom of your Higher Self so that you will complete your book more quickly, with deeper career alignment and personal fulfillment."

    **MIKAELA KATHERINE JONES**  Transformational Sound Artist, Higher-Self Conduit, and Author of *The Book of Light* and *The Little Book of Light*

"Coauthoring my book with my brother Jim through Modern Wisdom Press was a bonding experience we both treasure. As a published author of numerous academic papers, I knew how to write with my head but not my heart. The FLOW Method you'll discover in this book helped me dig more deeply into my inner experience and access a more personal style of writing that feels open and authentic. I would've laughed if you'd asked me about writing through my chakras before I began working with Catherine. That was about as foreign to Jim (a finance industry CEO) and me (a business professor) as possible. But her process worked! The Ideal Reader exercise brought clarity to our story. The words flowed easily onto the pages, and the feedback we've received about our book has been very encouraging. If you are ready to get your book into the world, I highly recommend working with Catherine and her team using the FLOW Method."

**STEPHEN GILLILAND, PHD** Claremont Graduate University Professor, Coauthor of *Pushing Up: What Twelve Months of Physical Challenges Taught Two Brothers About Connection, Leadership, and Purpose*

"As one of Catherine Gregory's clients and authors who successfully published a book, I can honestly say that it would not have happened without her expert guidance, the FLOW Method she developed, and her compassionate heart. The process that she so artfully describes in her new book, along with the many tools and her personal experiences as a writer, editor, publisher, and coach, are great gifts to anyone interested in writing or who wants to write that life-changing book they have not been able to manifest. No matter how many times you get stuck, suffer from imposter syndrome, or give in to the fears that inevitably show up on the path to publishing, Catherine's processes, suggestions, and support will move you through resistance to success and the realization of your dreams."

**BOBBI LAMBERT, PHD** Cofounder/President of Confidante, Inc., Author of *From Trauma to Healing: Seeking Solace and Safe Places to Fall*

# awaken into flow

### The Soulful Leader's Guide to Writing a Transformational Book

CATHERINE S. GREGORY

modern wisdom
PRESS

Modern Wisdom Press
Crestone, Colorado, USA
www.ModernWisdomPress.com

Copyright © Catherine S. Gregory, 2024

All rights reserved. No part of this publication may be reproduced or transmitted in any form or by any means, mechanical or electronic, including photocopying or recording, or by any information storage and retrieval system, or transmitted by email, without permission in writing from the author. Reviewers may quote brief passages in reviews.

Disclaimer: To protect the privacy of certain individuals, some names and identifying details have been changed. Neither the author nor the publisher assumes any responsibility for errors, omissions, or contrary interpretations of the subject matter within.

Published 2024

Paperback ISBN: 978-1-951692-43-8
E-book ISBN: 978-1-951692-44-5

Cover and interior design by KP Books
Author page photo courtesy of Van Dover Photography
Back cover author photo courtesy of Cherie Boylan

# Contents

Foreword . . . . . . . . . . . . . . . . . . . . . . . . . . . . . . . . . . . . . . . . ix
Introduction . . . . . . . . . . . . . . . . . . . . . . . . . . . . . . . . . . . . . . 1

| PART ONE | **The Calling** . . . . . . . . . . . . . . . . . . . . . . . . . . . . . . 5 |
| CHAPTER 1 | Now Is the Time . . . . . . . . . . . . . . . . . . . . . . . . 7 |
| CHAPTER 2 | The Inner Journey of Writing a Book . . . . . . . 19 |

| PART TWO | **The FLOW Method©** . . . . . . . . . . . . . . . . . . . . . 29 |
| CHAPTER 3 | The Energy of Flow . . . . . . . . . . . . . . . . . . . . . . . 31 |
| CHAPTER 4 | Engaging Your Energy . . . . . . . . . . . . . . . . . . . 45 |
| CHAPTER 5 | Follow the Breath . . . . . . . . . . . . . . . . . . . . . . 57 |
| CHAPTER 6 | Let Go of Fear . . . . . . . . . . . . . . . . . . . . . . . . . . 71 |
| CHAPTER 7 | Own Your Inner Wisdom . . . . . . . . . . . . . . . . . 87 |
| CHAPTER 8 | Write From the Heart . . . . . . . . . . . . . . . . . . . . 99 |

| PART THREE | **The Way Forward** . . . . . . . . . . . . . . . . . . . . . . . 115 |
| CHAPTER 9 | Know Your Why . . . . . . . . . . . . . . . . . . . . . . . . 117 |
| CHAPTER 10 | Know Your Reader . . . . . . . . . . . . . . . . . . . . . . 127 |
| CHAPTER 11 | Falling Out of Flow . . . . . . . . . . . . . . . . . . . . . 135 |
| CHAPTER 12 | Coming Back Into Flow . . . . . . . . . . . . . . . . . . 143 |

References . . . . . . . . . . . . . . . . . . . . . . . . . . . . . . . . . . . . . 149
About the Author . . . . . . . . . . . . . . . . . . . . . . . . . . . . . . 151
Acknowledgments . . . . . . . . . . . . . . . . . . . . . . . . . . . . . 153
Thank You & Additional Resources . . . . . . . . . . . . . . . . . 155
About Modern Wisdom Press . . . . . . . . . . . . . . . . . . . . . 157

To the Inner Creator within us all.

May we courageously share our talents, radiate our light, and create ripples of positive impact.

# Foreword

**IT WAS A THURSDAY** afternoon, and my introductory call with Catherine was in ten minutes. I had my entire speech prepared to tell her all the reasons we couldn't work together. I had done my research and knew she only worked with authors who wrote their own books. I would tell her how nice it was to meet her but explain that I wasn't a writer. The truth was that I had completely given up on writing my book, and the only reason I was having this call with Catherine was that a friend of mine had made the introduction.

I had previously spent two years with a ghostwriter trying to get my book into the world. Sadly, those two years failed to produce a book that felt authentic to my voice. I took a deep breath before the meeting started—it was time to let go of this dream of becoming a published book author once and for all.

Catherine and I started our call right on time at 3:00 p.m. Her warmth, professionalism, extensive publishing experience, and energy made me relax immediately, but not back down from my prepared speech. We spoke for about ten minutes before I started down my path of telling her I was not a good fit for her publishing company since I am not a writer. Two minutes into my speech, Catherine asked me, "What makes you think you are not a writer?" After I explained I am a speaker not a writer and offered other various excuses, she asked me one of the most powerful questions I have ever been asked: "How is not being a writer working out for you?"

I was stumped. She gently suggested that the story I was telling myself was the exact self-limiting belief holding me back. Even though I am an experienced executive coach and teach Fortune 500 executives the importance of recognizing the beliefs that get in their way, I could not see my own. I had been holding that I was not a writer since I first found out I had dyslexia as a high school student. I believed I was a speaker who was unable to write my thoughts.

In our work together, Catherine beautifully helped me see how wrong I was.

From that first Zoom call, she held the space for me to step into the possibility that I could write my book and utilize her framework to make the process joyful. I believe every person comes into your life for a reason, so I decided to dive in.

What I learned through our work together helped me change my story. The combination of structure, internal reflection, visualization, and process created the conditions for my book to pour out of me. It was unlike anything I had ever felt or experienced. I would wake up early in the morning excited to write and become immersed in states of flow in the writing process. I truly felt joyful writing my book.

Catherine's guidance was the key to unlocking something I never knew I had inside of me. The combination of touching my soul's work with the needed organization to make it come out effectively and with flow was pure alignment. If you had told me I would feel this way before meeting Catherine, I would have laughed out loud. Writing my book had not been in the realm of possibility for me, but the structure that Catherine has shared in this book transformed my reality and my life.

The FLOW Method creates the access point to your highest self in the writing process. It unlocks the barriers, elevates your mind, and creates an energetic flow to allow your inner wisdom to shine through. This book has an incredible combination of tools that speak with science to the intellectual mind and inspire the heart and spirit with soul-connecting practices that will remind you of your strength and wisdom that your future readers are waiting for you to share. Catherine guides you every step of the way to reach your potential as a writer and a person.

Writing my book with the FLOW Method was the first step in unlocking so many of my dreams. My book even won first place in the category of Inspirational/Motivational books from the Colorado Independent Publishers Association. After that incredible accomplishment, I decided to pursue getting my PhD, and now I have my Doctorate in Positive Organizational Psychology. My company Connected Executive Coaching has grown significantly since publishing my book to include a full coaching team and a research institute. Writing my book with Catherine's guidance was the first step in knowing that all my dreams were possible, and it gave me the ability to share my knowledge more broadly with the world. I'm now embarking on writing my second book.

If you are ready to become a published author and realize your dreams, I invite you to dive in and take this vital step to awakening your Inner Author. When you commit to the foundational practices you'll learn in this book, you'll be able to overcome the obstacles holding you back and be that much closer to having your long-awaited book in your hands.

— Jamie Shapiro, PhD
CEO and Founder, Connected EC, Author of
*Brilliant: Be the Leader Who Shines Brightly Without Burning Out* (Modern Wisdom Press, 2020)

# Introduction

I'VE FELT INSPIRED TO write this book ever since I *finally* published my first book, *Fertile: The Wise Woman's Guide to Pregnancy Success,* in 2018.

Publishing that book—and what I learned throughout the challenging journey of trusting my intuition and stepping into my calling—changed my life.

I went from being a newly divorced, distracted, and anxious mother of two teenagers (who was barely making ends meet) to a secure and financially successful solopreneur . . . in less than two years.

Take it from me: Writing a transformational book *will* change your life—if you are willing to embrace the inner journey and face the inevitable obstacles that come your way.

Thanks to my decades of spiritual practice and professional experience as an editor, energy healer, and transformational coach, I had all the tools I needed to navigate the self-doubt, subconscious fears, and other roadblocks that arise when writing a book.

And I really needed those tools!

It turned out that the transformational framework I had developed for my holistic healing practice—where I worked with women struggling to become mothers—was also the perfect process for me as I navigated the book-birthing journey.

Birthing any new creation requires both inward reflection and inspired action. We are bringing something brand-new into the world, which means we are birthing a brand-new version of ourselves, too. Fear of change is a human problem, and it will keep us stuck in our comfort zone—stagnating, procrastinating, perfecting, and making all kinds of excuses not to listen to our deepest callings. The lies that fear tells us sound logical, yet they are detrimental to our growth; they keep us stuck playing small and can prevent us from living a life that fulfills us and aligns with our purpose.

I wrote this book for soulful entrepreneurs and leaders who have an important message to share yet may struggle to bring that message into the world for any number of reasons. The FLOW Method© you'll learn about in this book has been tested and proven over many years by the dozens of published authors I've coached in our independent publishing venture, Modern Wisdom Press. It's for anyone who is ready to stop letting fear and other excuses keep them from shining their light and living their purpose!

Writing a successful book can increase your authority, expand your impact (and income), and elevate you as an expert. Writing a successful *transformational* book—one that positively impacts the lives of your readers—will do all of the above and have a beautiful ripple effect that brings more consciousness, well-being, and peace to the planet. And we all know the world needs more of that energy right now.

What sets the Modern Wisdom Press (MWP) book-coaching method apart from others is the exploration of the author's internal experience as they bring their book into the world. So many of the obstacles that authors encounter while writing a book happen subconsciously: fear of failure, fear of success, self-doubt, limiting beliefs, and impostor syndrome are just a few. At MWP, we guide our clients on an inner journey as they write their books, which helps increase self-awareness and presence so they can overcome obstacles, find flow, and enjoy the process of writing. This focus on intentionality and awareness is what leads our clients across the finish line and toward their dream of finally holding their published book in their hands.

Over the years, I've met with many brilliant leaders who really want what becoming a published author will bring them, but who have yet to commit to getting their message out to the world. I've even spoken with a few who admitted to secretly having a finished draft of their manuscripts on their computers! Why hide your wisdom and expertise? *Not* finishing your book deprives countless readers of a chance to make positive changes in their lives.

This is what happens when we let our subconscious thoughts, beliefs, and fears get in our way. For too long, my own excuses kept my fertility book from women who desperately wanted support—until I finally recognized the inner obstacles that were keeping me stuck and playing small. Our thoughts create our reality, and they have the power to keep us stuck—or soaring toward our purpose and destiny of writing a book that changes lives.

I wrote this book to be a light on your path as you embark upon the journey of becoming a published book author. In the pages ahead, you'll find more than a dozen personal practices to help you slow down and tune in to your inner experience, so that you can overcome the obstacles to sharing your wisdom and expertise through your book. Sometimes, these challenges are more practical in nature, like when you don't know how your book can help serve your goals or where to even start! You'll also learn the foundational steps that our published authors have used to birth their books into the world.

If you want to inspire your readers and change lives, this book will show you how to get out of your own way and into the energy of flow. Flow is a powerful state available to us all, and it can carry us forward in our writing, and into alignment with our highest vision for our lives. When you understand how to balance your intellect with your intuition and your mind with your heart, you'll discover the magic of flow, and writer's block will become a thing of the past. This inner journey of writing your book will bring you into the present and connect you with the creative flow of life itself.

Are you ready to begin the transformative journey of becoming a published book author? I'm so excited to help you get there. Let's jump in!

# PART ONE

# The Calling

# 1

# Now Is the Time

*If you commit to nothing, you'll be distracted by everything.*
JAMES CLEAR, *ATOMIC HABITS*

**WELCOME, FUTURE BOOK AUTHOR!**

Yes, I mean *you*, dear reader.

If this book has landed in your hands, I imagine you have a dream to share your wisdom and expertise by writing one of your own. You likely know that getting your book into the world will expand your reach, and that your message will make a positive impact.

As a soulful leader, you are guided by a deeper calling within that connects you to a higher purpose. You lead with empathy, authenticity, integrity, and have a desire to impact the greater good. You may be a healer or wellness practitioner, a teacher, parent, coach, consultant, founder, CEO, or business executive. But your title isn't what defines you. You are passionate about your work in the world and want to write a book because you know it will be of service. You likely cultivate a regular practice of staying present, centered, and intentional about how you spend your time, who you surround yourself with, and what you do with the precious hours of your days.

Whatever may be calling you to write your book, your core values are at the forefront of your decision-making. You bring intention to the many projects you choose and the roles you play. You've designed your work life to reflect the self-awareness and growth you've achieved in your personal life, and you see that the two are not separate. You embrace life as an ever-evolving opportunity for growth and expansion, and you have a feeling it's time to embrace your book journey as your next trip of transformation!

You know other published book authors are seen as authorities on their book's topic and are often invited to speak on their expertise—and paid well to do so. If written the right way, your book can help change lives, increase your impact and authority, and help you build a platform of fans who want more of your wisdom and expertise.

Yet for whatever reason, you've been stalling.

You're busy! I get it. I was too when I felt pulled to write my first book while juggling all the responsibilities of running my business, showing up for my clients, and parenting two teenagers as a newly divorced mom. Turns out I'm not the only one who has procrastinated on writing their book. Many published authors admit to having put off their commitment to finish their book until sometime "later" when their calendar opened up. News flash: Later isn't a day of the week! Years tend to slip by while life goes on as you wait for *later*.

If you're not a procrastinator, maybe you've started writing but aren't sure how to organize your thoughts and ideas effectively.

Or perhaps you lack clarity on where to start. You might be future-tripping with concerns about how to get your book published or what others will think about it. Or perhaps you're second-guessing your idea and wondering whether your book will even matter in the sea of books already on the market.

Whatever the reason you are here, I am passionate about setting you free, so you can get on to making the big impact you are here to make. This is the book I needed when I was spinning my wheels writing my first book. I wrote it to inspire and support you in accomplishing your important mission of becoming a published book author. And not just any book author, but an author of a book that will make a positive impact in your readers' lives—and ultimately, in your own.

### REMEMBERING MY OWN WISDOM

The method you'll learn in the coming chapters is the foundation of my coaching philosophy at Modern Wisdom Press, the transformational book coaching and publishing company I founded with my partner Nathan Joblin in 2019, after I wrote and published my first book.

Although I have a degree in journalism and spent the better part of two decades working as a professional editor and writer for international publishing companies, I found myself stuck and overwhelmed when writing my first book.

I was locked in my head—overthinking, second-guessing, and doubting my expertise, wisdom, and writing capabilities—which made the entire process dreadful. No wonder I procrastinated. My book project felt heavy.

My book idea was inspired by my personal journey to motherhood and the holistic fertility method I developed and used for fifteen years in my private healing practice.

As I sat down at the computer to write one day, I felt the typical sense of internal resistance arising. I noticed I was holding my breath. Then it dawned on me: I had practical tools that could help me get unstuck. They were from the method I'd developed to help hundreds of women overcome the inability to conceive, gestate, and birth a baby. I applied the holistic process to my journey of conceiving, gestating, and birthing a book—and eureka! It worked. (You'll hear more of this story in a bit.)

This method has since helped dozens of authors get unstuck and birth their transformational books into the world. By using these potent tools, our busy clients are able to overcome obstacles, find clarity, and write their books in just a handful of weeks.

### AN INNER TRANSFORMATION

Whenever we embark upon a big endeavor—especially writing a book that inspires positive change in our readers—courage and introspection are needed. Know that when you find yourself stuck, there's a ripe opportunity for personal transformation.

Take a moment to zoom out and look at the big picture of where you were before you started down the path leading to where you are today. Think back on the many trials and tribulations that resulted in your personal growth and transformation, leading you to this moment now, wanting to write a book.

When I think back to my life before writing my first book and compare it to my life now, I'm amazed at how much has changed. From personal experience, I know that becoming a published book author requires clarity, focus, determination, and a commitment to succeed.

When you are willing to embrace the inner journey of transformation that happens when you write a book, it's absolutely possible to do it in a way that feels fun and joyful—and won't lead to burnout.

Contrary to all of the bust-your-ass book-writing myths, you do not need to suffer, take a sabbatical, or spend months ignoring your other life commitments to finish your book.

As the statistics will tell you, writing a book takes commitment and follow-through. According to an article in *Business Insider,* it's estimated that 200 million Americans dream of writing a book—yet only 3 percent finish their manuscripts, and of those, only 20 percent go on to become published. (Epstein 2002) But don't let that scare you! None of that means you must struggle in the process.

When you understand the energy of flow and how to awaken yourself *into* flow, writing and finishing your book doesn't have to be an arduous feat that feels impossible. Of course, it will require effort, but when you're in flow, writing your book can *feel* effortless.

This book will show you how to find flow . . . consistently and consciously.

## AN ACT OF SERVICE

When you see your book as an act of service, inspiring and transforming the lives of those who read it, you are much more likely to commit and stay motivated to finish it. In fact, one of the most rewarding aspects of writing a transformational book is the accomplishment you feel from creating an impact for your readers.

Your future readers are waiting for you to finish your book! Maybe, like me, you even wish you'd had the book you're working on when you were younger. If you have an inspiring message, story, or transformational process that you know can help others, can you now see that the world is waiting for your book and your book is waiting for you to write it?

It's time, my friend, to share your wisdom and expertise, and help others on their paths by writing your book. When you do, you'll discover another reward: who you become in the process. Accomplishing this goal will bring you new levels of personal insight, confidence, and clarity, which will further support you in giving voice to your visions and sharing your gifts with the world.

## THE POWER OF VISUALIZATION

How did you feel when I called you "future book author" at the beginning of this chapter? What feelings came up for you? Excitement? Joy? Dread? Fear? Disbelief?

Can you envision what your life will look and feel like when your book is physically tangible and in your hands? Can you see your book in your readers' hands, making the impact you dream of in lives across the globe?

Please take a moment right now to pause and experience this vision. Imagine a future scene of yourself as a published book author. After reading this paragraph, close your eyes and allow yourself to dream. Let all the creative details come into focus. Where are you? What are you doing? Who are you with? What are your readers saying to you about your book? How do you feel in this scene, now that your book is no longer just a dream but a manifested reality in the world? Once you get a tangible sense of your future self as a published author, open your eyes and take a moment to write down all the details, including your emotions and how you felt.

Hold on . . . did you actually close your eyes and do that mini guided visualization in the last paragraph? If not, promise me you'll come back to it before you move on to the next chapter.

Visualization is a powerful practice that will support your success in finishing your book. World-class athletes, speakers, performers, and visionary leaders frequently use visualization to achieve their goals and desired outcomes. So do our published authors. You'll have more opportunities to practice the art of visualization in the chapters ahead.

## EGO + SOUL = SUCCESS

Our minds have the power to create our reality. Therefore, we have a choice to make: We can stay small and stuck in all our excuses for why we have yet to finish our book, or we can examine the thoughts and beliefs that have created our current reality and do something about them.

To overcome writer's block, overthinking, and second-guessing, and finally find the clarity and flow to enjoy the writing process, we must be willing to look within as we write our books. This inner journey will be familiar territory if you've intentionally embarked upon any personal growth experience.

When we look in the mirror by practicing self-awareness, we are more equipped to see our human limitations—and the ego-driven fears and desires behind them. This knowledge is immensely helpful as we embark upon the often challenging path of writing a book. When we feel "called" to write a book that will inspire and change lives for the better, we can trust that it's our Higher Self or soul calling us to fulfill our purpose. When we are stalled or stuck as we pursue that calling, we can bet that's our confused ego.

Though the ego often gets a bad rap, there's nothing inherently wrong with it. Your ego is that unique part of you, your personality and psyche, that guides your actions in the world and can uniquely express your soul's desires. The ego can get confused by fear, especially fear of change, and put the brakes on our progress. Or it can get sidetracked by visions of fame and set us down a path that's out of alignment with our higher purpose. The healthy, mature ego and soul are a great team. They need each other, in fact. And when they work together in harmony, beautiful things happen—like life-changing books!

## BUSTING THE MYTHS

There are countless myths out there about what it takes to write a book. Maybe one of your limiting beliefs is that it takes years to write a good book, and you just don't have the time. These untruths can perpetuate avoidance, fear, and procrastination, stopping many life-changing books from ever coming into existence.

As a transformational book coach inspired to bring more consciousness and healing to the planet, I am here to help bust these myths! You can and will overcome your conditioned beliefs about the book-writing journey (whether collective or personal) when you bring awareness to your inner experience as you birth your book into the world.

Here are some truths about writing a life-changing book that you'll learn about in the coming chapters . . .

- Writer's block is a myth. Feeling stuck is 100 percent avoidable when you bring intention and awareness to your whole self—mind, body, and soul—during the writing process.
- You have an internal operating system that can turn your confusion into clarity, your doubt into confidence, and your wisdom and expertise into a magnet for more income and impact.
- Flow happens when you let go of the excuses, limiting beliefs, and subconscious fears that may be holding you back from blossoming into your full potential.
- You can trust your intuitive guidance and inner wisdom

by learning how to distinguish the competing voices in your head.
- By getting to know your Inner Editor and Inner Author, you'll learn ways to find balance and harmony between your intellect and intuition, so you can enjoy the process of organizing, writing, and bringing your book into the world.

The chapters ahead will guide you through practices to help you bust through whatever is holding you back and find more inspiration and confidence as you bring your book to life.

## WHAT YOU'LL LEARN IN THIS BOOK

I've organized the book's chapters into three sections.

Part One addresses the common challenges faced on the journey of writing a transformational book and how to finally overcome them.

Part Two shares the FLOW Method, a proven process for overcoming obstacles and finding flow to write your book. This method is used by all our transformational authors at Modern Wisdom Press. Each of the FLOW Method chapters includes guided practices, which you may like to read aloud and record so you can play them back and be guided along by your own wise voice.

And finally, Part Three will show you how to build a solid foundation for your book, helping you identify your goals, understand your readers, and customize your plan for finishing the book you're meant to write.

## FLOW WRITING

At the end of the chapters, you'll also find short flow-writing prompts to help you examine your internal experience and find momentum in your writing. If you don't already own a journal, please buy one and dedicate it to your flow-writing practice.

These prompts are designed to help you access deeper insight and awareness on your journey to becoming a published author, and they will aid you in writing your chapters when the time comes. Though typing your answers on a screen is okay, the physical experience of using a pen or pencil on paper is more conducive to "releasing" and clearing internal space for more energy to flow, which is the point. The prompts will encourage you to pour your thoughts onto the page in a timed exercise.

Writing without editing—without concern for punctuation, grammar, style, or whether it's good or not—awakens flow. This is how we train our brains to get through obstacles like perfectionism, procrastination, second-guessing, rewriting, and overthinking: We write with abandon to clear the clouds of confusion, so that clarity can shine through. This is where you will meet your Inner Author, who lives within the energy of flow. This is where you'll discover your inner wisdom and the higher purpose of your book and allow flow to guide your way forward.

Practicing flow writing disengages your Inner Editor, sometimes referred to as the *inner critic*. However, there's an appropriate time and place for your Inner Editor in the book-writing journey, so don't worry—you'll learn about that, too.

I've practiced this simple form of flow writing since I was a preteen, when I got my very first diary. It was the old-school kind with a lock and key, so maybe that gave me the sense of freedom I needed to express all my thoughts and feelings safely on the page.

I'm encouraging you to set yourself free, too. If you can find a journal or notebook with a lock, and that's what you need to write uncensored, then do that. Otherwise, know that these exercises are meant for your eyes only. They are designed to deepen your connection with yourself, helping you bring more awareness and compassion to your inner experience, which creates more space for creativity to flow.

These flow-writing prompts are designed to prime you for writing the first rough draft of your manuscript. Trust me, when perfectionism had me stuck rewriting every paragraph of my book, I recovered using this flow-writing practice, so I know it works. It helps you get some experience under your belt in what writing with flow feels like. It's incredibly liberating when you give yourself permission to play on the page, allowing whatever words that show up to be there, with no pressure to make it "good."

If you believe your book will serve those who need your knowledge and expertise, then to serve, you must trust your inner wisdom and allow the flow of creative expression to move through you. When you tap into that energy, you become the channel for the words to pour through you. Flow writing is how our authors write first drafts of manuscripts in mere weeks, not years. This method helps us access the knowledge, intelligence, and wisdom that is inherent within us. To be able to write with flow, we must disengage the inner critic and trust that by moving out of our own way (the ego's limiting thoughts and beliefs, that is), we will be able to birth the book that is calling to us.

The more time you give to these flow-writing practices, the easier it will become to write your book's chapters. Trust the process. When you begin with your inner journey, your book-writing adventure will naturally start to align with your vision, your values, and your greater purpose of serving more people with your important message.

I know you've got this. So let's begin!

---

## FLOW-WRITING PROMPTS

The best way to answer these prompts is to read through the questions first, then set a timer for five minutes and start writing, keeping your pen moving (or your fingers typing) until the timer is done. Don't worry about grammar, punctuation, spelling, or whether it's good writing. Just allow words to come until the time is up. This is how you begin to trust yourself and allow your writing to flow.

- Which myths or stories about writing a book have held me back?
- Where did I first hear them?
- Do I still believe them? Why or why not?

## 2

# The Inner Journey of Writing a Book

*Your outer journey may contain a million steps; your inner journey only has one: the step you are taking right now.*
**ECKHART TOLLE, *THE POWER OF NOW***

**I USED TO FEEL** ashamed of how long I'd been working on my book. Years had gone by, and I had nothing to show for it.

Can you relate?

Maybe, like me, you were inspired by an idea for a book, yet over time you lost momentum, and the energy for it fizzled out.

I had knowledge and expertise that could really help my readers, yet when it came to writing my book, I'd start, stall, and often prioritize other "more important things." When I finally did sit down to write, I'd write in circles, confused about how to organize my thinking and effectively share the methodology that would not only change lives but birth new ones! I would feel embarrassed when friends and family asked how my book was coming along.

I was in my own way and I knew it, but I couldn't figure out how to get unstuck.

I knew how to write well enough, so I wasn't sure why my book-writing saga was so dang hard. Before I opened my private healing arts practice, I had worked as a writer and editor for several prestigious publications. Writing had been my profession, so why was I stuck when it came to writing this book? It didn't make sense to my logical mind. The cycle of sitting down to focus on my book, then feeling overwhelmed, procrastinating, losing steam, putting it aside, and almost giving up went on for years.

Until one early January morning, when I woke up suddenly from a vivid dream. I had been holding my book in my hands. I could feel the weight of it, the texture and colors of the cover, and I could even see the title. It felt so real. I didn't know if I was dreaming or not. Then I heard the words *"Now is the time."* When I awoke, I knew in that moment that no matter what, I would trust that guidance. That would be the year I'd stop making excuses and finally get my book into the hands of my readers.

## BUSTING THROUGH FEAR AND LIMITING BELIEFS

After that dream, I also knew I needed accountability, so I hired a coach to help me stay on track with my writing deadlines. I invested in my commitment to prioritizing my book, and with that outside support, I finally found momentum—and eventually, a big dose of clarity.

Having a number of tools for personal growth and transformation, I dug deeper into why I had been stuck for so long. I realized that the obstacles I'd faced trying to write my book were mostly internal. They were limiting beliefs and subconscious fears, some more conscious than others, and they were masked by some pretty logical-sounding thoughts:

*Other projects are more important right now.*
*I'll get started on that this weekend . . . next week . . . next month.*
*There are already so many books; does mine even matter?*
*What if my book flops and people judge me?*

And this fear surprised me the most . . .

*What if I'm successful?*

You may already be aware of your subconscious fears to some degree and know which thoughts or beliefs aren't serving your growth. If not, the prompts at the end of the next chapters will help you uncover the root of your excuses for not moving forward.

Once I saw which limiting beliefs and subconscious fears were in my way, I needed to dive deep and meet them head-on.

My fear of success, it turned out, was rooted in a childhood fear of being seen and the subconscious belief that "success" meant I would be so busy I wouldn't be available for my children . . . just like my successful, hard-working father wasn't always available for me. Our childhood wounds will hold us back until we face them. By nurturing our inner child with tender, loving care and presence, we can address subconscious fears that might still be holding us back in life.

Despite having fifteen years of subject-matter expertise and countless professional case studies of success that I knew could inspire my readers, my self-doubt and subconscious fears were driving my distraction, procrastination, and debilitating perfectionism.

Every time I sat down to write, my Inner Editor would engage, critiquing every word, every comma placement, and the bones of each sentence. So before I could get through a single paragraph, I was typing, deleting, typing, deleting, cutting and pasting . . . and thoroughly exhausted. No wonder I had been getting nowhere fast all those years! (You'll learn more about working with your Inner Editor in Chapter 6.)

## TRUSTING SIGNS FROM THE UNIVERSE

Once I addressed my self-sabotaging obstacles and put the tools you'll soon learn into practice, I found myself in a state of flow. Chapter by chapter, mere weeks later, I was wrapping up the final paragraph of my book. It was Mother's Day.

I knew that especially on that holiday, the women I was writing to were hurting. They wanted to be mothers and needed my book sooner rather than later, so I decided to roll up my sleeves and embark on a path of self-publishing. It took several months to find the right experts to help me design the book's interior and cover, edit the manuscript, and get it published.

Serendipitously, I launched my e-book into the world on Labor Day that year. That's when it struck me. I had been "gestating" a book for women who longed to be mothers. Further alignment came exactly nine months after writing that last chapter, when I held the paperback for the first time. Mother's Day. Labor Day. Nine months later . . . my "book baby" was finally in my arms!

My dream had come true. I'd learned how to awaken flow by choosing to see my book journey as a personal growth opportunity. I had uprooted the subconscious fears and beliefs that were keeping me stuck writing in circles. I had discovered a balance between my intellect and intuition, my Inner Editor and Inner Author, and my ego and soul to bring my wisdom into the world through my book.

It felt like a cosmic wink. I'd answered the call of gestating and birthing a new creation into the world, and discovered a potent method that could help others in the process. The Universe was dropping all the clues, showing me how the creative process of my holistic fertility method could be applied to birthing just about anything new into the world. When four of my trusted colleagues asked if I could help them write their books, I realized I had to say *yes*!

I admit I never saw that work as a book coach and publisher coming; I just trusted my intuition as my compass and said *yes* when the Universe kept nudging me forward. Considering the blood, sweat, and *years* it took to birth my first book, the irony is not lost on me. I don't want other aspiring authors like you to suffer as I did. And the great news is, you don't have to!

## YOU'RE NOT ALONE

What has surprised me most in my book-coaching work is how many brilliant leaders and subject-matter experts get stuck in their limiting beliefs and subconscious fears as they begin to write their books. Despite their self-awareness or years of training or experience in their field, every single author we've supported has encountered obstacles of one kind or another on the journey to finishing their book.

When Diane, a wellness researcher, came to us, she admitted she'd started writing her book on her own, but she wasn't sure her writing was good enough. She'd been trained to rely on research for everything she'd ever written before, so she often quoted other experts to back up her points. As a result, her writing felt disconnected and dry. She knew she needed to write more authentically to connect with readers and make the impact she wanted to make, yet she lacked the confidence that her years of expertise or unique voice was enough. When she finally embraced her inner wisdom and shared her vulnerability through personal stories, her content became much more relatable. Once her book was published, she took the great storytelling from it onto corporate stages and her speaking career took off.

Our clients Melissa and Mark are cofounders of a successful consulting business and longed to coauthor a book. They kept making excuses that they "weren't ready." They were busy consultants, after all. Their to-do list kept growing and other projects were a priority, even though they both admitted they saw this pattern happening year after year. They knew their framework was transforming teams and organizational culture and that writing a book could help them expand their impact and make the difference they really wanted to make. Melissa even admitted she got "pissed off" when she saw her colleagues announce their new books.

Melissa and Mark finally saw their procrastination pattern and decided to commit. By prioritizing their book despite their full calendars, they found that the outside accountability was key to making the time to align with their vision and write their book. Within two months, they had a finished manuscript. After publishing their book, their business began thriving more than ever before.

Our client Leah had the time to commit to writing but feared she was "spinning her wheels," not sure if her content was making sense or connecting to her ideal audience in an engaging way. Once she embraced her professional expertise and owned her inner wisdom, she found clarity about her book's organization, and her writing began to flow. She finished her manuscript with more confidence than ever, eventually launching a new speaking career using her book as her calling card and creating a new revenue stream of international retreats. She knew that by writing her book, she would be fulfilling her purpose and serving her future readers, but she didn't see her new ventures of speaking and hosting retreats (and the joy those offerings would bring her) until after she wrote the book.

All these aspiring authors overcame their obstacles and now have books that are helping them build communities of loyal fans who want more of their transformational offerings.

## WHY COMMITMENT MATTERS

When my clients begin working with me, the first thing they do is sign and date a commitment statement. This is, most importantly, a promise to themselves, a powerful few paragraphs they read aloud so that I can hold them accountable for their commitment to finishing their book and becoming a published author.

As you embark upon the next stages of awakening flow in the coming chapters, it's important to examine and acknowledge your commitment to finishing your book. If you're inspired and ready to act on your dream of being a published book author, sign the statement on the following page and keep it somewhere you'll see daily. This will be an important step of accountability to keep you moving forward. (See *Thank You & Additional Resources* for a downloadable version.)

## COMMITMENT STATEMENT

I, _____, commit to following through on writing and publishing my transformational book. This commitment is essential to my forward momentum and success.

I choose to take action toward birthing my book every single day, including cultivating or maintaining a daily meditation/presencing practice. I believe in my capacity to complete my book manuscript, and I'm willing to put in the work required to prioritize this goal.

By engaging the tools of the FLOW Method from this book, I will cultivate a deeper connection to my inner wisdom and creative process to access more clarity and allow my book to flow through me with ease and joy. My commitment to this process will empower me to face and overcome the obstacles and resistance that may arise along the journey.

I commit to setting aside time daily to engage in the tools and practices to help me find flow in writing my book. I understand I am ultimately responsible for my success in completing my manuscript, and my commitment to the FLOW Method will help lead me there.

These practices will require me to dig deep at times. I'm willing to embrace this journey and be open to its gifts as I commit to taking action to write this book and make a difference in the lives of those who read it. It all begins today.

_____
YOUR SIGNATURE

_____
DATE

© MODERN WISDOM PRESS

## SLOW DOWN AND TUNE IN

I invite you to take your time, as you read this book, to digest the concepts and engage with the practices and prompts offered in each chapter. In our fast-paced hustle culture, we often rush from task to task, skimming the surface content of life and missing opportunities for deeper insight, clarity, and meaning. How often do you take time to slow down, reflect, and savor the moments of your day?

Confusion, dear reader, is an egoic phenomenon. We walk around feeling lost, overwhelmed, or confused about things in life mostly because we haven't slowed down to listen to our inner wisdom. The answers we seek are already within us. There are times when we need outside accountability or guidance (like from a book or a good coach or therapist) to help steer us out of the dark. But most of the time, what we really need is to *slow down and tune in* to our own inner wisdom to find the clarity we seek.

Clarity comes from your soul. To access your inner wisdom, aka the voice of your soul, you must intentionally pause and create enough breathing room to hear your soul's whispers and nudges.

When you embrace your inner wisdom and the inner journey of writing a life-changing book, you'll find clarity, joy, and much more ease in the outer journey!

---

## FLOW-WRITING PROMPTS

The best way to answer these prompts is to set a timer for five minutes per question and start writing, keeping your pen moving (or your fingers typing) until the timer is done. Don't worry about grammar, punctuation, spelling, or whether it's good writing. Just allow the words to come until the time is up. This is how you begin to trust yourself and allow your writing to flow.

- ⊙ What fears or limiting beliefs might be holding me back from finishing my book?
- ⊙ When have these fears showed up in my life before now?
- ⊙ Am I willing to be honest and explore these blocks to set myself free?
- ⊙ If I feel any resistance to exploring my inner experience, including my emotions, thoughts, beliefs, and fears, why is that?

# PART TWO
# The FLOW Method

# 3

# The Energy of Flow

*Just as a wave is a movement of the whole ocean, you are the energy of the cosmos. Don't underestimate your power.*

**DEEPAK CHOPRA**

**ANYTIME YOU BIRTH SOMETHING** new into the world, you undergo a transformation. You are birthing a new version of yourself as its creator. You must be willing to be transformed as you write your book. To be successful, you must let go of your old identities, your fears, and whatever else might be holding you back from your inevitable transformation into a published book author.

Seeing this journey of transformation through a holistic lens, the FLOW Method invites us into the present moment to look within. The practices ahead will help you slow down overthinking and release self-doubt and confusion. You'll learn how to balance your logic and intuition, trust your inner wisdom, and write from the heart.

When you embrace the energy of transformation, you attune to your Higher Self, or your soul: that deepest part of you calling you to step up and birth your creation into the world.

When I recall the journey of writing my first book, I remember eventually understanding that I was subconsciously resisting this transformation. I had chalked it up to writer's block, the convenient excuse we have for externalizing our inability to find clarity and flow in our writing. But when I decided to look deeper, I saw that the real blocks keeping me stuck were rooted within my own internal energy.

## EVERYTHING IS ENERGY

To awaken flow, you first must understand the science of energy.

*Energy is the life force that flows through all things.*

As a meditation instructor and intuitive healer, I find that working with energy and guiding others in understanding and using their energy to awaken flow comes naturally to me. When I left my career in the magazine publishing industry to launch my holistic fertility practice, I became certified in several energy healing modalities and studied with both Eastern and Western practitioners and traditional healers.

In the Ayurvedic and Yoga traditions, this life force energy is called Prana. In other Asian traditions, this energy is called chi (or qi) and flows through pathways called meridians within our bodies. Acupressure and acupuncture in Traditional Chinese Medicine and qigong, a mindful movement practice, utilize these meridians to circulate qi through the body.

In the West, scientists have conducted extensive research over the past century to better understand how energy impacts our lives. Research has shown that energy vibrates at different rates or frequencies, measured in hertz (Hz), and that positive and negative emotions generate different vibrational frequencies. (Halliday 2014)

In-depth research by the HeartMath Institute, for example, has shown the connection between emotions and the electromagnetic field generated by the heart. Their findings suggest that positive emotions, such as love and gratitude, create coherent heart rhythms that can enhance our health and well-being.

Dr. Masaru Emoto's famous water crystal experiments show a similar result. He exposed water samples to different intentions, such as love, gratitude, and hate, and then froze the samples to observe the resulting ice crystal formations. The water exposed to positive intentions formed beautiful, symmetrical crystals, while water exposed to negative intentions formed disorganized and distorted crystals. Because the human body is primarily composed of water, these findings have changed our understanding of how thoughts and emotions can impact our health.

Quantum physics takes our understanding of energy even further, helping us see how our energy can impact others. The phenomenon known as entanglement shows how one energy source can blend with and conform to another.

In the journal *Physics Essays*, physicist Amit Goswami showed that entanglement affects people, meaning one person will conform to the energy of the other person. (Goswami 1989) For example, when one person is a healer, whose cells are vibrating at a higher level, the client's cells become entangled with those of the healer, and their energy is lifted.

The good news is you don't have to be an "energy healer" to be able to lift the energy of others. Because our emotions, thoughts, and words are energy too, we have the power as authors to uplift and inspire our readers with our writing. To do this, we first must become aware of our energy and the emotions that impact it. Only then will we be able to elevate our energetic vibration and express that on the page. We'll dive more into this concept in Chapter 8.

## WHAT EXACTLY IS FLOW?

The word *flow* has several definitions.

When I use the word *flow*, I am talking about the term *flow state*, which describes a mental state in which a person is completely focused on a single task or activity. They are directing all their attention toward the task, and as a result, they don't experience many thoughts about themselves or their performance. Some people refer to this informally as being "in the zone."

The concept of this kind of flow comes from the field of positive psychology, which is the science and study of life's positive qualities—the things that help humans thrive. Mihaly Csikszentmihalyi, who was an influential part of the movement, coined the term. (Csikszentmihalyi 2008)

During a state of flow, several changes take place in the brain. Studies have shown that the dopamine reward system plays an important role.

Dopamine is a neurotransmitter that supports feelings of motivation, pleasure, and reward. It can also help suppress bodily sensations such as hunger. People in a state of flow have higher levels of dopamine, which could explain why they might not notice that they are hungry or tired. (Cristol 2024)

You might be surprised to learn that the flow state isn't some elusive state we need to chase. Flow is our natural way of being when we come into the present moment. Flow states happen when we're not caught up in our busy minds, thinking about the past or the future.

*Flow seen through this lens, in essence, is presence.*

Being in the flow feels like a dimension of "no time" because it happens in the eternal now. Flow makes efforting feel effortless. Flow invites synchronicity too, magically lining everything up in our favor. We experience it more often when we are actively engaged and immersed in an activity with concentration and focus; this most often happens because we've stopped our incessant thinking and have come into the present moment.

Most of us have likely experienced a flow state when we're doing something we enjoy. When our minds are focused on one enjoyable activity, our train of thought slows down, and we merge with the moment at hand. Making love, art, or a delicious meal can all bring us into flow. Top athletes, artists, musicians, and other creatives utilize flow states to achieve their visions and goals. Flow states help humans break records, create masterpieces, and manifest long-awaited dreams.

Flow states can also bring feelings of ecstasy, joy, and bliss, and a sense of being attuned to Universal energy. This cosmic or Divine experience makes our writing feel easy, as if we were downloading the inherent creative expression of life itself.

To access flow as we write, we must learn how to harmonize our personal energy with the Universal energy around us. This means we are not really awakening flow (which is already present)—we are *awakening ourselves into* flow.

This is the foundation of the FLOW Method that you'll learn about next. By understanding how to tap into the treasured "state of flow" when writing, I found calm and clarity and was able to finish my first book, which I'd been trying to write for years, in a matter of weeks. The FLOW Method will help you get unstuck, so you can finally get your book into the world, too.

When your writing feels easy and you lose track of time, you are in a state of flow. The words simply "flow" through you onto the page. You become the conduit for cosmic intelligence and your soul's voice, aka your own inner wisdom. Colorful ideas and new insights arrive, and you experience a heightened sense of clarity that naturally weaves your sentences, paragraphs, and chapters together like a gorgeous silk tapestry.

Most of our authors at Modern Wisdom Press start and finish writing their manuscripts within just five weeks. I know that sounds incredible, but this kind of magic is possible for you, too!

## LIKE ENERGY ATTRACTS LIKE ENERGY

If you have felt called to write your book, or you simply have a "knowing" that it's time, I believe that is the voice of your soul tapping you on the shoulder. These callings are what we might refer to as intuitive guidance. They come to us as messengers to help us align with our higher purpose. Our souls are here in these human bodies to evolve, and our internal hunches can be trustworthy guides on the path to our personal growth and transformation.

In my book-coaching work, I invite my clients on a personal journey: going within to balance their energetic systems as they are writing their books. This inner work is the secret to their success in overcoming obstacles and completing their manuscripts. When you understand how to work with your energy using the practices in this book, you'll be able to ditch self-doubt and overthinking, and find the clarity to bring your book to life, too.

My client John is a successful financial planner who dreamed of writing a book about his unique method of helping his clients with retirement plans. His methodology isn't based on the traditional financial strategies that most planners follow, but they have contributed to big successes for his clients and are the reason for his practice's recent expansion and growth.

Yet as John was digging into a chapter deadline, he became gripped by self-doubt. "What if all the traditional financial planners are right and I'm wrong?" he worried. "What if my peers mock me or my writing isn't smart enough?" And he began to spiral, questioning his book as well as his entire reason for doing the work he loves, around which he had built his life and business.

Thankfully, John had enough self-awareness to recognize the train of negative thoughts as impostor syndrome, a common derailer for many aspiring authors. He stepped away from his computer and took a moment for self-reflection, employing a few of the tools you'll learn, and he was able to derail the negative train of thoughts and get back on track and into flow with his writing.

You see, whenever we're stuck or unable to move forward with a creative project, it helps to understand the nature of energy and how it naturally seeks flow. We can work with our own internal energy to overcome obstacles and help bring forth new, creative expressions from a place of flow.

From an energetic perspective, whatever we are seeking is seeking us, too. By awakening into flow and harmonizing your energetic vibration with that of your book, you magnetize it to you in a tangible form.

Like energy attracts like energy, which is why I am a huge proponent of visualization, especially on the book-writing journey.

If you are new to visualization, this practice of going within to find clarity and inner guidance will likely be profound. I've seen this many, many times working with authors.

By visualizing your desired outcome (like you hopefully experienced in the first chapter) and the feelings associated with that future state, you are activating the magnetic principles of the Law of Attraction, which is a powerful form of manifestation.

Almost everything wonderful I've manifested in my life within the past ten years (my two books, my devoted life partner, our purpose-driven business, our dream clients, our soulful dog and cat, our beautiful home in the mountains, and my loving relationships with our adult children) has come from intentionally aligning my energy with my desired outcome and visualizing it on repeat. I had to see it in my mind and *believe* it all was possible *first* before I could see it become a reality. This is the power of creative visualization. It is a potent practice that anyone can adopt to bring more flow and manifestation magic into their lives.

*When we are in flow, we feel content, creative, and connected to something larger than ourselves.*

In flow, we attract what we desire without struggle. That is my wish for you, dear reader, as you write your book.

### THE FLOW METHOD

Because everything is made up of energy, and you now see that your thoughts, emotions, and words are energy too, let's talk about how the FLOW Method will help you write your book.

Energy naturally wants to flow. Imagine the momentum of a river and how the water is constantly finding its way around obstacles as it effortlessly flows downstream. Your writing can become like water, finding a way to flow through you and onto the page.

Understanding where your energy gets stuck and learning how to remove obstacles and unblock the flow within you is the secret to successfully finishing your book. So let's dive in.

The tools I use to coach aspiring authors on how to awaken into flow are wrapped up in a nifty acronym that spells, you guessed it . . . FLOW.

>     Follow the breath.
>     Let go of fear.
>     Own your inner wisdom.
>     Write from the heart.

## F: FOLLOW THE BREATH

What does breathing have to do with writing, you may wonder? Well, our breath is an amazing tool that can bring us into the present moment, and that is the only place where we can access flow. Flow comes to us when our minds aren't busy ruminating about the past or worrying about the future. We are right here, in the moment—in the flow.

When we slow down and bring our awareness to the breath, following the inhale and exhale for just a few cycles, something pretty spectacular happens: Our firehose of thoughts begins to slow down, and we are able to arrive in the present moment, aligning and harmonizing our personal energy with the source of Universal energy.

This powerful practice of paying attention to the breath is the basis of many meditation and mindfulness techniques. When we follow the breath, we get out of our heads and into the now. We are no longer clouded by overthinking, second-guessing, or trying to "think" our way through our writer's block (or any kind of stuckness). The clouds of confusion part, the light shines in, and we ignite clarity and creative energy that wasn't previously accessible.

You may already have a meditation or mindfulness practice or other tools like conscious breathing for dropping back into the present moment. Excellent! I recommend using these before and after you write. You'll find additional presencing practices to add to your toolbox in the chapters ahead. Find what works best for you, create your own daily routine, and make it a habit to do those practices before you write. To enjoy the writing process and awaken into flow, you must come out of your busy mind and back into the present moment.

We can't really stop all our thoughts, but we can stop our attachment to them and the trap of overthinking, which commonly happens when we're trying to organize the content for a book. We can get stuck in our heads, sometimes utterly confusing ourselves. This is why we absolutely must slow down and get into the present moment to access flow.

### L: LET GO OF FEAR

I've already shared some of the subconscious fears and limiting beliefs that were holding me back in my writing journey. I used to think I was the only one with such debilitating hang-ups. Yet every single author I have coached experiences self-doubt somewhere along their book-birthing process. We're human, and the energy of fear is something we all experience in some form or another. Negative thoughts and limiting beliefs are often rooted in the energy of fear. Fear also shows up in covert ways when we are writing, hiding behind perfectionism, procrastination, and impostor syndrome.

In Chapter 6, you'll learn how to discern the voice of fear and discover tools to help you move through these saboteurs.

## O: OWN YOUR INNER WISDOM

All the life experience, wisdom, and knowledge you have acquired, which have led you to your work today, are beautiful gifts for your future readers. Your voice matters. Your unique perspective on your topic matters. Your book will resonate with those who are meant to find you, attracting your ideal readers—those who seek the exact transformation you're offering in the exact way you're communicating it—no matter how many other books on the topic are out there.

Our inner wisdom speaks to us through our intuition, which is sometimes referred to as a "gut instinct"—an inner knowing that helps us stay aligned with our soul's higher purpose and calling. We hear this inner voice in quieter moments, like the voice in my dream that spoke the words "Now is the time" as I was holding my future book in my hands. Trusting our intuition uncorks the well of our inner wisdom.

Practices like meditation, quiet time in nature, and the flow-writing exercises in this book are great ways to hear our intuitive voice and receive its guidance.

In my experience, sometimes the voice of my intuition is loud and clear, like someone speaking in my head, and other times it's more of a feeling sense that comes from deep within: a full-body YES.

Encouraging and listening to our intuition can guide us out of confusion, doubt, and fear, and into clarity. Trusting and owning our inner wisdom as we write will bring our authentic self-expression onto the page.

## W: WRITE FROM THE HEART

Answering the call to write a book that inspires and transforms your readers is a courageous act of service.

Writing from the heart means having compassion for our readers and ourselves. We come to the page with a servant's heart. When we write from the heart, we magnetize those who need our words. They find us relatable and human. The more authentic and transparent we can be in our writing, the more our readers begin to trust us.

For many of us, writing from the heart feels vulnerable. We are "opening" ourselves up to our readers, sharing our truths and our deepest transformations, which led us to our work today.

To be able to express yourself more authentically and deeply as you write—and to be seen by your readers in your vulnerability—can be scary. You have to shift your mindset from being a "perfect" expert or authority who has it all figured out to being a human who's struggled and made mistakes and figured out a solution that readers will benefit from knowing. Being vulnerable makes your writing much more relatable and human. When you write from your heart, you tap into a well of creativity and authenticity that shines on the page and attracts the ones who are meant to find you.

---

### FLOW-WRITING PROMPTS

Please do yourself a favor and do not skip over these prompts. By nurturing your inner journey of writing a book, you'll pave your way to finding flow when it's time to write your book's chapters! Set a timer for five minutes per question. Savor the time for your inner reflection. Write without stopping, without worrying about grammar or whether it's good writing or not. New information may arrive for you on the page. This will help you access your inner wisdom and discover more clarity and guidance as you write your book.

- What are the current practices I use to access my intuitive guidance?
- What insights or intuitive guidance have I already received about my book?
- Do I trust this guidance? Am I doubting or resisting this guidance in any way?

# 4
# Engaging Your Energy

*May what I do flow from me like a river,
no forcing and no holding back...*
**RAINER MARIA RILKE**

**PUBLISHING A BOOK IS** a lot like giving birth. I can say this because I've birthed two babies and now two books! (Okay, I will not lie: Birthing a baby is *much more* physically, emotionally, and spiritually demanding, and home birth continues to be the most powerful and empowering experience of my life. But I digress.)

Regardless of whether or not you've given birth to a baby, my point here is that like with pregnancy, when we want to birth a book, we have an intangible creation inside of us that isn't yet fully formed. This creation needs our full presence, attention, and nourishment to gestate and grow and become a sovereign entity that lives outside of us. Before it arrives Earthside in our hands, we are its nurturer, its creator. And to deliver our creation into tangible form, we must embrace our whole selves—our physical, mental, emotional, and energetic selves—and see the process as the holistic journey it is.

As energetic beings, we are designed with an innate operating system called the chakras, which move energy internally through our physical body and externally out into what is known as our energetic body. Modern science still lacks the tools to measure the subtle energy that makes up the chakra system, yet the HeartMath Institute has conducted extensive scientific research showing bioelectromagnetic interactions in and between people, which may be the basis of our energetic bodies. Their research has shown that the electromagnetic signal produced by your heart is registered in the brainwaves of people around you. (McCraty 2004)

We can also look to the historical interpretations of the chakra system documented for thousands of years in India. According to ancient Indian yogic traditions, it is understood that we have seven main chakras inside the body, which are invisible energy portals situated along the spine. (Mitchell 2023) These centers are responsible for our physical, emotional, and spiritual well-being. In Sanskrit, chakra means "wheel" or "disk." Each chakra moves energy into and out of our bodies, emitting a unique energetic expression or frequency out into the world.

When balanced and open, the chakras allow energy to flow through us, nourishing our organs and internal systems while connecting us to the world and the greater Universal source of energy beyond our physical bodies. Imbalanced or blocked energy flow through these main chakras results in physical and emotional imbalances, impeding our connection with Universal energy and the experience of flow as we write.

By understanding how this energy system works, you'll become empowered to bring awareness to the obstacles that are keeping you out of flow—and move through them with the practices at the ends of the chapters ahead. Understanding how to support your internal energy flow through the chakra system will help you find flow in your writing, too.

## THE SEVEN CHAKRAS

Each of the seven main chakras within the physical body is associated with a different color and function. When these chakras are in balance, we feel healthy, happy, and "in the flow" of life. But when they become imbalanced, we experience blocked or excessive energy manifesting in physical and emotional symptoms—including feeling stuck and out of alignment with our calling and higher purpose in life.

It's incredibly powerful to balance your energy and overcome potential obstacles that impede flow.

Even though they aren't physically visible, I describe the chakra centers as horizontally spinning spirals of energy, like wheels along the spine, with the spinal column being the hub of each wheel. Starting at the base of the spine or tailbone is the root chakra, and all seven energy centers are positioned along the spine, up to the crown of the head.

The obstacles in our internal energy flow, or blocks within our chakras, often manifest in symptoms (physical, mental, and emotional) and are the root cause of what we might refer to as "writer's block."

As you move through each step of the FLOW Method in the chapters ahead, you'll find guided practices to explore and assess the flow of energy in each of the main seven chakras within your physical body. These begin with a guided breathing practice, followed by flow-writing prompts related to each chakra.

From my own experiential understanding of awakening into flow, working with the chakras is the most direct way to bring self-awareness to your energy flow and obstacles on the book-writing journey. When our authors admit to second-guessing or overthinking as they write, these practices aid their awareness of their inner blocks and help them move through them to realign with their calling and experience more flow in their writing.

When you take the time during the process of writing your book to tend to your inner world, especially through the guided visualizations and flow-writing prompts, two important things happen. One, you can identify and uproot underlying thoughts and patterns that are blocking your forward momentum. And two, you activate the power of your Inner Author simply by writing (without editing) about something that is *not* intended as content for your book.

As you practice flow writing through these prompts, you can let go of perfectionism and learn how to write from the heart with honesty, authenticity, and vulnerability, which will make your content engaging and help your readers trust you.

Before you move into the FLOW Method chapters coming next, it's important to understand these seven main chakras and how energy expresses itself as it flows through each center.

**Root Chakra: Get Grounded**

The root chakra, also called *Mūlādhāra* in Sanskrit, is located at the base of the spine. It is associated with feeling grounded, safe, and secure. This center is also responsible for our survival instinct. A balanced root chakra can root or ground us into our bodies and into the present moment. Balancing its energy flow will help us to feel more embodied, present, and safe. Bringing awareness to the energy flowing through our root chakra will help us receive the nourishing, supportive energy of the Earth and get out of our busy, overthinking minds.

| | |
|---|---|
| CROWN CHAKRA | SAHASRĀRA |
| THIRD EYE | ĀJÑĀ |
| THROAT CHAKRA | VIŚUDDHA |
| HEART CHAKRA | ANĀHATA |
| SOLAR PLEXUS | MAṆIPŪRA |
| SACRAL CHAKRA | SVĀDHIṢṬHĀNA |
| ROOT CHAKRA | MŪLĀDHĀRA |

### Sacral Chakra: Get Creative

The sacral chakra, or *Svādhiṣṭhāna* in Sanskrit, is located just below the navel. When balanced, it fuels your ability to create, feel pleasure, and manifest your dreams. In my healing work, I refer to this part of the body as the womb, regardless of gender or whether the client has a physical uterus. In Traditional Chinese Medicine, this part of the body is referred to as Dan Tien. We are all inherently creative, and when our sacral chakra is open and in balance, we increase our capacity to feel and express our creative ideas and are inspired to bring our visions into reality.

### Solar Plexus: Set Boundaries and Commit to Inspired Action

The solar plexus chakra, or *Maṇipūra* in Sanskrit, is located in the upper abdomen and is associated with our personal will, confidence, and ability to take action. When you start writing a book, count on the Universe to throw obstacles onto your path to test your commitment! Your aging parent needs your attention more than usual, your child is home sick from school, or your new client is now demanding the time that you had blocked off for writing. No doubt there will be real-life demands and challenges that you must address along the journey of writing your book. You must protect your commitment to finish your book by maintaining clear boundaries—otherwise, life's unexpected hurdles can take you and your book dreams down.

### Heart Chakra: Overcome Fears and Limiting Beliefs

The heart chakra, known as *Anāhata* in Sanskrit, is the bridge that connects the lower three chakras to the upper three chakras. Having an intention to open your heart strengthens your emotional connection to yourself and others. For the book-writing journey, an open heart will deepen your connection to your readers and open you up to a higher, Universal source of energy and wisdom. Fear is what closes your heart, and it can show up in small anxieties or in large, debilitating ways. Working with your heart chakra helps you explore your underlying fears and limiting beliefs, so you can move through them, opening up to the energy of unconditional love to fuel your writing.

### Throat Chakra: Clarify and Express Your Voice

The throat chakra is referred to as *Viśuddha* in Sanskrit, and it is situated in the center of the throat. When balanced, this chakra allows you to express your voice confidently and speak your truth authentically. Unblocking the flow of energy through this chakra helps you to connect with your readers as you write. When you're able to express yourself by speaking and writing clearly and genuinely, you are paving the path to building trust in your readers and increasing your relatability.

### Third Eye: Trusting Your Intuition

The third eye chakra, or *Ājñā*, is located between the eyebrows in the center of the forehead. This is the energy center that helps you hear your intuitive voice or inner wisdom and see beyond the illusion of this physical reality. Your intuitive guidance flows from this energy portal, and it's always available if you slow down and simply tune in. When you practice creative visualization, you are strengthening the energy of your third eye and intuitive capacity. We learn to trust in the unseen, in gut feelings, in our inner "knowing." When balanced and open, this chakra helps us tap into the more psychic aspects of our intuition, known as the *Clairs*.

These are called clairvoyance (the ability to see), clairaudience (the ability to hear), clairsentience (the ability to feel), and claircognizance (the ability to know), from beyond the veil that separates our human selves from our higher spiritual selves (Dale 2009).

### Crown Chakra: Connecting to Divine Inspiration

The crown chakra (*Sahasrāra* in Sanskrit) is associated with our intellect and intelligence. It sits at the very top of our heads. When balanced and open, the crown chakra connects our intelligence to Universal or greater life force energy beyond our physical bodies, egos, and personalities.

You may refer to this as your soul, your Higher Self, the Universe, God, or nature. An open crown chakra allows you to channel wisdom from your own intellect and beyond. You're able to see beyond your ego and become a channel for Divine flow. By opening the crown chakra, you can remember the higher purpose of your calling to serve through the pages of your book. Your ego—and its unique expression through your body, psyche, and personality—enables you to manifest your soul's calling. These two forces are at play in bringing your inherent wisdom and unique gifts into the world.

## BALANCING AND ALIGNING THE CHAKRAS

With awareness of your energy flow through each chakra, you can balance and align all seven centers to download Divine wisdom as you write. In some ancient Indian spiritual traditions, this life-force energy is referred to as Shakti or kundalini and is believed to lie dormant at the base of our spine, or root chakra. On a spiritual awakening journey, the intention is to bring kundalini all the way up through the chakras, in order to have an experience of enlightenment or a sense of oneness with the Universe.

Although this book is not about achieving spiritual enlightenment, when you work with the chakras and with kundalini or energy flow moving through you, you have the potential to reach higher levels of energetic frequency and consciousness. When you do, you increase your resonance with readers and become a channel for wisdom and words to flow through you, making your experience of writing exciting and joyful.

## HOW DO THE CHAKRAS AFFECT YOUR WRITING?

When your energy centers are blocked or out of balance, here's how that may show up on the book-writing journey.

- **Root Chakra Imbalance**—Feeling confused, ungrounded; anxious thoughts
- **Sacral Chakra Imbalance**—Lacking creative ideas or insight; uninspired
- **Solar Plexus Chakra Imbalance**—Procrastination, distraction, self-doubt
- **Heart Chakra Imbalance**—Writing that feels impersonal or overly intellectual
- **Throat Chakra Imbalance**—Limited self-expression, holding back your authentic voice
- **Third Eye Chakra Imbalance**—Lacking clarity or trust in your intuition/insight/inner knowing
- **Crown Chakra Imbalance**—Disconnected from a higher perspective so you can't see beyond your egoic desires

When the chakras are open and energy is flowing effortlessly through, they help you to . . .

- **Root Chakra Balance**—Feel safe and grounded in the present moment and trust yourself.
- **Sacral Chakra Balance**—Ignite your creativity, inspiration, and ability to manifest your dreams.
- **Solar Plexus Chakra Balance**—Boost your self-confidence, commitment, and will to follow through.

- **Heart Chakra Balance**—Write with vulnerability, connecting with empathy and compassion for your readers.
- **Throat Chakra Balance**—Express your thoughts clearly and use your voice authentically.
- **Third Eye Chakra Balance**—Hear and trust your intuitive guidance and own your inner wisdom.
- **Crown Chakra Balance**—Open to higher guidance, becoming a channel for Universal wisdom to flow through you.

As you move into the next section of the book, you'll be guided and prompted to get to know your own energetic system and chakras—to balance the energy flow within you.

By combining the four practices of FLOW—Follow the breath, Let go of fear, Own your inner wisdom, and Write from the heart—you will lay a solid foundation for success as you begin organizing and writing the chapters of your book.

As you answer the following prompts, practice being unconditionally loving and gentle toward yourself. Answer them honestly, from your heart.

## FLOW-WRITING PROMPTS

Set a timer for five minutes for each question. Answer the following questions by writing without stopping, allowing the words to pour out. This exercise isn't about good writing; this is about being honest with yourself and setting your truth free onto the page. There's magic in this practice. The secret is to keep writing without stopping. See what comes. You are embarking upon the inner journey of writing your book. This exercise will free up space within you, and when you commit to these inner journey prompts, your book writing will become much more accessible as you slowly awaken more flow.

- Based on the descriptions of the chakras in this chapter, which of my chakras might be out of balance or blocked?
- How is this showing up in my life or in my book-writing journey?
- Why do I think this energy is out of balance?

# 5
# Follow the Breath

*Breath is the bridge which connects life to consciousness.*
**THICH NHAT HANH**

**WRITING A BOOK IS** naturally a mental process. We must engage our intellect, organize our thoughts, and be laser-focused on stringing our words together coherently to keep our readers engaged. Writing logically, focusing, and meeting our deadlines requires us to bring our intelligence to bear. Yet if we're *only* focused on the mental aspects of the journey, we can come up against some pretty gnarly obstacles that threaten our success altogether. This is why we must balance our intellect with our intuition, and our minds with our hearts. This is how we find flow.

Our first step to awakening into flow begins with the breath.

**F: FOLLOW THE BREATH**

Many of us wait to be "inspired" to start writing. We want to feel filled with ideas, clarity, and energy to write before we begin.

But what if we could find inspiration in the breath itself?

From an energetic perspective, our breath gives us energy and connects us to life. We can't live without it. The word *inspiration* comes from the Latin word *inspiratus*, which essentially means "breathe into." To "inspire" means to breathe in or to inhale. Through our breath, we meet the external magical forces that give us life, fill us with energy, and animate us with ideas and creativity. When we follow the breath, we can find inspiration.

As you bring your attention to your inhale and exhale, you naturally let go of overthinking and come into the present moment. Your breath is an energizing tool that is ever ready to bring you into flow, into inspiration. Breathing mindfully—with awareness—is also known as "conscious breathing."

We breathe all day long—and all night as we sleep—without thinking about our breath. Breathing is an automatic, essential process like digestion that our bodies require to stay alive. Yet when we stop taking the breathing process for granted and instead breathe with awareness, we naturally bring more oxygen into our body and may notice an increase in both energy and inspiration.

> Take a minute now to simply follow your breath, focusing your attention on your inhale and exhale. Set a timer for one minute and close your eyes to really tune in.
>
> Try it now, and then come back to this page.

How'd that go? Were you able to keep your attention focused on the breath? Did your mind wander? Did you notice physical sensations in your body that you hadn't previously been aware of? Or do you now feel a slight tingling or have a heightened sense of mental clarity and focus? By following the breath, you are accessing a free tool that you can use any time, day or night, to slow an anxious or overthinking mind, bring you into the present moment, and access a portal to more inspiration, focus, and clarity.

What we often don't realize is that when we are trying to focus on the perfect words to write, we may be holding our breath or breathing quite shallowly. No wonder we don't feel inspired!

When we tune in to our breath, we can become more aware of our thoughts. When we spend time following the breath, the fast train of our thinking begins to slow down, and we can become a witness to our thoughts instead of getting caught up in them. We can let our thoughts float by like clouds in the sky. We're able to connect with our larger sense of awareness, which is vast like the sky. This is the eternal now, this present moment, which is where flow exists. It's always there; we just have to slow down enough to access it.

**POWER IN THE PAUSE**

Slowing down and tuning in to your inner experience (including your thoughts, beliefs, and emotions) is an invaluable tool for gaining momentum on the journey of writing your book. And yes, it's a paradox. You might wonder, *How will I finish my book if I slow down?* Trust me, dear reader, there is power in the pause.

By attuning your energy to the present moment, you naturally fall into flow. This is where magic happens and your writing becomes supercharged with creativity. Being in the present moment means we let go of our thoughts and beliefs—our internal stories about what our experiences have taught us, as well as the conditioning that keeps us stuck. Presence is where we access "beginner's mind"—a state of experiencing the present moment from a childlike state of not knowing—which allows new thoughts and creative ideas to flow. By releasing our preconceived ideas about what we think we know, we get out of our own way and open ourselves up to new possibilities.

You don't have to be an energetically sensitive person to benefit from these practices. Authors writing on topics such as money management, executive leadership, and workplace well-being have all used these practices to get unstuck.

## BEING VERSUS DOING

Because slowing down paradoxically supports your writing momentum, reflective practices can help you get out of your head and into your heart.

> **BOOK BIRTHING TIP**
> **MAKE SLOWING DOWN SACRED**
> Create an altar for your Inner Author that inspires your vision and commitment. You might include a candle, items from nature, photos of loved ones, or something that symbolizes your book's purpose.

Even though you are actively "doing" something when you are writing, by committing to slowing down—whether through mindfulness, a guided meditation, or a breathing practice beforehand—you are cultivating presence and the art of simply "being." This, in turn, will open the door to even more intuitive guidance and creative inspiration.

Ideally, you will intentionally slow down before you sit to write and bring awareness to your breath while you are writing. It's also great to create bookends to your day, engaging in at least twenty minutes in the morning and twenty minutes in the evening for your slowing down practice. But even if it's just ten minutes per session, when you commit to making it a daily routine, you increase your chances of successfully finishing your book.

## CHAKRA BREATHING PRACTICES

Using the breath to bring awareness to the flow of energy through each chakra will help you sense where energy may be blocked and help balance and open these energy portals within. At the end of each FLOW Method step, you'll find a chakra breathing practice and flow-writing prompts that are meant to be done together. Doing so will help you bring more awareness to your internal experience, ultimately bringing more support to your book-writing journey. I encourage you to focus on one chakra at a time to gain an experiential awareness of your energy there before moving on to the next chakra.

As you learned in Chapter 4, the balanced root chakra helps you feel safe and supported, the sacral chakra sparks your creative ideas and expression, and the solar plexus chakra empowers you to take action by committing to your calling. Using your breath to unblock the energy that flows through these lower three chakras will help you feel more grounded, embodied, creative, and confident as you write.

**CHAKRA BREATHING PRACTICE**

**ROOT CHAKRA**

I encourage you to record these breathing exercises in your own voice and then play it back to yourself, so you can close your eyes and deepen into a guided meditative experience. For each of these practices, begin by finding a comfortable seat, perhaps in a chair or on a cushion on the floor. Make sure that your knees are level with your hips, so as not to put unnecessary pressure on your lower spine.

> Close your eyes and begin to tune in to your inner experience by focusing on your inhale and your exhale. Follow your breath in through the nostrils, imagining that it's flowing all the way down into your belly. Soften your abdominal muscles and allow the breath to fill your pelvic bowl. As you exhale,

imagine the breath moving down, out of your body, out of the tailbone or the feet, flowing down into the Earth. Visualize roots extending from your physical body deep into the Earth, spreading out in all directions, grounding you into the support of the Earth. As you exhale, let go of anything that isn't serving you. Breathe it down into Mother Earth, who is a great transmuter of energy, taking whatever you release and reforming it, like compost.

Do another round of this inhale through the nose into the belly, and exhale out of the body through the tailbone or feet. This time, on the exhale, visualize a long taproot extending down from your body into the center of the Earth. Follow the exhale all the way down, anchoring yourself in the Earth's core. This root receives nourishment from the Earth in the form of light. Breathe that light up from the center of the Earth, through all your roots, and into your physical body, through your feet or your tailbone. Repeat this inhale and exhale cycle again, exhaling down your taproot into the Earth, and then inhaling light from the Earth's center into your root chakra at the base of the spine.

Visualize energy flowing into this center as a spiral, moving clockwise on the inhale and counterclockwise on the exhale, expanding down, out of the body, into the Earth. The color associated with the root chakra is red, so envision a red light glowing within you as you breathe into this energy center. On your inhale, this ball of light spirals in a clockwise direction, receiving energy from the Earth. As you exhale, imagine releasing energy from the root chakra in a counterclockwise direction, back down into the Earth. Breathe this way for several minutes. When you begin to feel a sense of openness in this chakra, you will feel grounded, secure, supported, and more present in your body.

Notice whether you feel any resistance or blocks in this energy center—if you do, continue to use the inhale and exhale to breathe energy from the Earth up into this chakra. This pattern of breathing will help to clear and balance your root chakra.

When you feel complete, open your eyes and stretch, drink some water, and take a moment to reorient yourself into your environment.

Now is the perfect time to answer the flow-writing prompts below.

### ROOT CHAKRA FLOW-WRITING PROMPTS

Set a timer for five minutes per question and start writing, keeping your pen moving (or your fingers typing) until the timer is done. Don't worry about editing, grammar, punctuation, or spelling—or whether it's good writing. Just allow whatever words to come. This is how you begin to trust your Inner Author to simply flow.

- In what ways do I distract myself from slowing down and tuning in to my inner experience?
- Why might I resist slowing down?
- How do I currently reduce stress or anxiety? Why is this working for me? Or why not?
- How does my body feel as I'm slowing down and paying more attention to my inner experience?
- What does my body want me to know right now?

### SACRAL CHAKRA: IGNITING YOUR CREATIVE POTENTIAL

We are all inherently creative beings. By opening the sacral chakra energy center, we can access our natural manifesting power and unblock the flow of creativity to bring something new into the world. I've seen it again and again with authors who are up against blocks writing their books. When they do this guided practice to open and balance this chakra, this creative energy center within, they open up the energy flow of their writing, and their creative expression comes through in all kinds of new ways.

**CHAKRA BREATHING PRACTICE**

**SACRAL CHAKRA**

Begin by finding a comfortable seat, perhaps in a chair or on a cushion on the floor, making sure that your knees are level with your hips, so as not to put unnecessary pressure on your lower spine. Record the meditation in your own voice for the deepest experience.

> Close your eyes and begin to tune in to your inner experience by focusing on your inhale and your exhale. Follow your breath in through the nostrils, imagining that it's flowing all the way down into your belly. Soften your abdominal muscles and allow the breath to fill your pelvic bowl. As you exhale, imagine the breath moving down out of your body, out of the tailbone or the feet, flowing down into the Earth. Visualize roots extending from your physical body deep into the Earth, spreading out in all directions, grounding you into the support of the Earth.
>
> Do another round of this—inhale through the nose into the belly, and exhale out the body, through the tailbone or feet. This time, on the inhale, breathe light up from the center of the Earth, through all of your roots and into your physical body, through your feet or your tailbone. Repeat this inhale and exhale cycle again, bringing white light from the Earth's center up through your root chakra at the base of the spine into the sacral chakra, illuminating a ball of orange light in your womb space.

Visualize energy flowing into this center as a spiral, moving clockwise on the inhale and counterclockwise on the exhale, expanding down, out of the body, into the Earth. Notice any sensations as you breathe in and out of the sacral chakra for several cycles. Do you sense any blocks? Breathe light into the sacral chakra and breathe out any blockages, down through the root chakra and into the Earth.

Continue to breathe into this energy center until you feel a sense of warmth and appreciation. Can you send a breath of gratitude to this part of you that has manifested so much into your life already? Allow your womb space and sacral chakra to fill up with the breath of gratitude, repeating the cycle of breath until you feel balance and openness through this energy portal.

When you feel complete, open your eyes and stretch, drink some water, and take a moment to reorient yourself to your environment.

Now is the perfect time to answer the flow-writing prompts that follow.

---

### SACRAL CHAKRA FLOW-WRITING PROMPTS

After doing the Sacral Chakra Breathing Practice, answer the following set of questions using as much detail as possible. Remember, these prompts are designed to help you write with flow, so no editing! Set a timer for five minutes and allow yourself to write uninhibited for this set of questions. It's good to keep your pen moving or your fingers typing for the entire timed exercise, even if you end up writing "blah, blah, blah" when you don't have words. Soon, more words will come.

- ⊚ What is something I've recently manifested in my life that I feel happy or proud about, and why do I feel this way?

- What were the steps I followed to achieve this reality?
- How did my mindset impact my ability to bring this into reality? What thoughts was I thinking throughout the process?
- What support did I receive to help me manifest this?

Take a moment to breathe in some gratitude to your sacral chakra for its creative energy and your ability to manifest your desires!

## SOLAR PLEXUS: DEFINING YOUR BOUNDARIES

Situated in the upper abdomen, above the navel and below the ribs, the solar plexus chakra helps us know and express our personal will and purpose. An open and balanced solar plexus chakra empowers us to commit to our calling, take inspired action, and achieve our goals. We can use the power of this energy center to build confidence and strengthen boundaries around our commitments. When life throws a curveball our way, and we miss a writing deadline or two, this energy center strengthens our drive and helps us find a way to follow through with our plans.

**CHAKRA BREATHING PRACTICE**

**SOLAR PLEXUS**

Sit somewhere comfortable, such as in a chair or on a cushion on the floor, making sure that your knees are level with your hips, so as not to put unnecessary pressure on your lower spine.

Close your eyes and begin to focus on your breath.

Follow your breath in through the nostrils, softening your abdominal muscles and allowing the breath to fill your pelvic bowl. Visualize roots extending from your physical body deep into the Earth, spreading out in all directions, anchoring you in the support of the Earth.

Do another round of this—inhale through the nose, into the belly, and exhale out of the body, through the roots, into the Earth. Let go of anything that isn't serving you. Let the Earth transmute whatever you want to release, recreating it, like compost. On your next inhale, visualize breathing in light from the Earth's center up through your root chakra, illuminating that red ball of light. Breathe in and breathe out of that energy center before inhaling up into the sacral chakra. Visualize the breath illuminating an orange ball of energy there, breathing in and out, before moving into the solar plexus chakra.

As you focus your awareness on the solar plexus chakra, just below the rib cage, imagine the breath flowing into this energy center as a yellow spiral of energy, moving clockwise on the inhale and counterclockwise on the exhale, expanding down, out of the body, into the Earth. On your inhale, this ball of light spirals in a clockwise direction, receiving energy up from the Earth. As you exhale, imagine releasing energy out from this chakra like rays from the sun, surrounding yourself in a cocoon of golden light, extending out from the body by two or three feet.

Continue this pattern of breath for several minutes, breathing energy into the solar plexus from the Earth, and exhaling energy out, into a cocoon of golden light surrounding your entire physical body. When you begin to feel a sense of openness in this chakra, you will feel empowered, energized, protected, and inspired. Notice whether you feel any resistance or blocks in this energy center, and if you do, continue to use your inhale and exhale to breathe energy from the Earth up into this chakra. This pattern of breathing will help to clear and balance your solar plexus chakra.

When you're ready, open your eyes and stretch, drink some water, and take a moment to feel your feet on the floor.

Now is the perfect time to answer the flow-writing prompts below.

---

### SOLAR PLEXUS FLOW-WRITING PROMPTS

Set a timer for five minutes per question and start writing, keeping your pen moving (or your fingers typing) until the timer is done. Don't worry about editing, grammar, punctuation, or spelling—or whether it's good writing. Embrace and trust your Inner Author to simply flow.

- Where do I give away my power when it comes to my personal commitments?
- How do I dim my own light or play small?
- What boundaries do I need to put into place to protect my commitment to finish my book?

Take a moment to breathe in some appreciation for your solar plexus chakra and its energy flow of personal empowerment.

As you wrap up the first step of the FLOW Method, take note of how you feel. Engaging the lower three chakras in the body helps ground us to our physical experience as human beings—with egos, in bodies, on Earth. Hopefully you've gained new insight and an experiential understanding of your energy flow through these three chakras. To experience a guided visualization recorded in my voice, you can access my Limitless Creative Flow guided meditation here: www.ModernWisdomPress.com/limitless-creative-flow.

In the next step, you'll experience the heart chakra, which transmutes our fears and is a bridge between the three lower chakras and the three upper chakras. The heart chakra is a powerful portal that helps us integrate and express our soul's desires through our grounded, mature, egoic selves.

# 6

# Let Go of Fear

*Avoiding danger is no safer in the long run than outright exposure. Life is either a daring adventure or nothing.*

**HELEN KELLER**

**THOUGH CHANGE IS THE** only constant in this human experience, most of us have an underlying fear of change, whether we're conscious of it or not.

The most fundamental purpose of fear of change is to keep us alive. Our nervous system is wired to look out for danger and seek ways to keep our physical organism safe. As we fall asleep at night, the intelligent nervous system might be reviewing our day and assessing our overall level of safety, saying something like "Well, I'm still alive after what I did today, so let's just keep doing that to stay safe." This is how we get stuck in our comfort zones and develop an unconscious resistance to change of any kind, especially big change.

When our nervous system perceives danger, its fight-or-flight response dumps adrenaline into our body to help us escape a predator or a life-threatening situation. This same stress response can also get triggered by much less threatening situations, like an impending deadline, a difficult conversation, or a traffic jam that will make you late to a meeting.

These kinds of stressors aren't life-and-death, but our bodies don't know the difference and send all the same signals for escape and avoidance. Transitions like birthing a new creation or a new version of ourselves bring change. From the perspective of our nervous system, change means a potential threat to our safety. So it's no surprise that we experience anxiety, self-doubt, and fear (whether conscious or not), and tend to put the brakes on a big change, even when it's something we dream of doing like becoming a published author.

To get out of your comfort zone and step into your calling, you must be willing to die egoic deaths along the way. By letting go of your fears—and with them, the old versions of yourself that no longer serve you—you become willing to transform. If you truly want to write a book, give a TED Talk, or shine your light in a brighter way—aligning with your purpose, whatever that may be—you must welcome the opportunity to recreate yourself. When you do, you will likely bump up against your innate resistance to change. Hello, subconscious fears and limiting beliefs. But once you understand why they exist, you can use techniques to soothe your nervous system as you embrace and evolve through change, taking one inspired step at a time toward your calling.

When you birth a book into the world, you are stepping into a new identity and role as a published author. With that title comes expectations: A book author is perceived as someone who has intelligence, expertise, knowledge, and authority. Many are seen as thought leaders in their fields.

Published book authors speak on stages, give keynotes, take interviews with the media, and are often sought out for their subject-matter expertise. Does this kind of public exposure excite or scare you? Though many aspiring authors would love to expand their impact and influence in these ways, it's natural that some of those ideas might trigger anxiety, especially if being in the spotlight or speaking to audiences is not something motivating you to write your book.

As I explored my resistance and blocks during my own writing process, I realized that my fear of public speaking was at the root of my procrastination and perfectionism. I imagine my subconscious voice of fear probably sounded like "If writing a book means I have to be in the spotlight and stop hiding in the background where it feels safe, no thank you!" I had to dig deep to find the root of my "fear of being seen" and work with the childhood stories that came with it.

## PROCRASTINATION, PERFECTIONISM, AND IMPOSTOR SYNDROME

When we have an underlying fear of the changes that come with being a published book author, we might find ourselves putting the brakes on our momentum and progress. Through my book coaching, I've found the top three most common ways fear shows up for aspiring authors is through procrastination, perfectionism, and the infamous impostor syndrome.

Procrastination-based thoughts or excuses might sound like . . .

> *I don't have the time to write my book right now.*
> *Other priorities are more important.*
> *I'll make time to work on that next week . . . next month . . . next year.*
> *I need to get my PhD (or another credential or certification) to be taken seriously as an author.*

> There are already a ton of books on my topic, so why spend time writing another one?

Procrastination can keep us from ever starting. Or if you have begun writing, you might find yourself opening Instagram or a news channel in another browser during the times you're supposed to be getting words on the page.

If you aren't distracting yourself with cat videos or other forms of clickbait, maybe your underlying fear shows up as perfectionism. Perfectionism is tricky. It can appear that you're committed to your book project and working hard to get it done. But really, you're stalling your progress by overthinking and reorganizing chapters, or moving things around as you write, trying out new ideas and rewriting each sentence before you get to the end of a paragraph. Say hello to your Inner Editor! This part of you can endlessly sabotage your forward momentum with perfectionism.

As a recovering perfectionist myself, I share this with full transparency: I caught my Inner Editor taking over throughout this book-writing experience. Awareness of our fears and the way they show up is the first step to overcoming them! Using the tools of the FLOW Method will help ease your anxieties and allow your Inner Author to shine.

**IMPOSTOR SYNDROME**

When you find yourself second-guessing your expertise, your knowledge, your education, your credentials, or the whole idea of writing a book, say hello to impostor syndrome! Feeling like a fraud or that you aren't "good enough" is a common subconscious fear that can hold you back. Impostor syndrome makes us doubt ourselves despite our greatness, and it threatens to stop even the most accomplished among us. Our inner impostor might think thoughts that sound like . . .

> *Who am I to write a book?*
> *Other people have written great books on this topic; mine will never be that good.*
> *Nothing I want to share sounds that unique, interesting, or smart.*
> *What if I'm really just a fraud?*

Maya Angelou, a literary legend, talked about the impostor feelings she experienced each time she published a book: "I have written eleven books, but each time I think, 'Uh oh, they're going to find out now. I've run a game on everybody, and they're going to find me out.'"

Angelou was nominated for the Pulitzer Prize and won three Grammys for her spoken-word albums (plus numerous other awards), yet she still had the feeling that deep down, she didn't have a clue what she was doing.

Does knowing that even the most accomplished writers and creators second-guess themselves help ease your own self-doubt?

We can give ourselves a break when self-doubt rears its ugly head. We don't have to be perfect or have it all figured out to be able to help others with our books.

I too experienced my share of impostor syndrome writing this book. Though it's much more manageable now that I'm aware of it and I have tools to move through it, it still shows up. However, I know that facing my own limiting beliefs has helped me step out of my comfort zone and ultimately transform my life, and that continuing to face these fears will further help me grow and transform.

If you are serious about your commitment to serve by writing a life-changing book, then, my friend, it's time to examine whatever may be holding you back.

## YOUR INNER EDITOR (THE PERFECTIONIST) AND YOUR INNER AUTHOR

Just as a human pregnancy requires a sperm (masculine) and egg (feminine) to begin fertilization, we need both feminine and masculine energy to create and birth anything new into the world. We all possess both energies within us, regardless of our gender identity. Some of us may express more feminine energy and others more masculine energy, but one is not better than the other.

Like yin and yang, the two complementary principles of Chinese philosophy, when we aim to balance the masculine and feminine energy within us, we are more likely to enjoy a fruitful and sustainable creative process. Especially when it comes to writing a book.

I'm not a neuroscientist, so please forgive my simplification of how these energies are expressed through our very complex, intelligent brains. This is how I've learned to work with the polarities of masculine and feminine energies when it comes to writing a book.

The left (or masculine) side of the brain is the source of our logical, linear, organizational thinking. It is a necessary ally when we're pulling together all the ideas and content we want to share and organizing it to create an outline for our book. I call this part of the brain our Inner Editor. The Inner Editor brings logic, critique, and order into the process of writing.

Oh, do I know this side of my brain well! As a professional editor for twenty-five years, I've created deeply grooved neuropathways while editing, and my sense of organizing and scanning content for what's working and what's not is well honed. Very well honed, in fact. The dark side of an overactive Inner Editor is debilitating perfectionism. So in writing my first book, I found myself editing as I wrote, rewriting every sentence, which is not at all productive when it comes to finishing any piece of writing, let alone a book. Hence the feeling of writing in circles. And I'm not alone! High achievers are often perfectionists. This is a common thing our authors struggle with, too.

Perfectionism is tricky because it feels like we are deeply committed to the highest-quality product, but it can actually be fear holding us back from ever bringing forth the thing we really want to birth!

Perfectionistic thoughts that pop up while we are writing might sound like . . .

> *Oh, I could rewrite that sentence to sound more clever.*
> *I'm not sure this paragraph/chapter title/subtitle makes the impact I want. I'll rewrite it now.*
> *I should rethink/reorganize these subsections/ chapters again.*

And then . . .

> *Oh, maybe they were better like they were before!*

And on and on the critiquing goes . . .

There's a time and place for the Inner Editor to do its thing, and it's *not* when we're in the process of writing. That's the job of our Inner Author. The right side of our brain is associated with our feminine energy and intuition and is the realm in which our Inner Author lives. This is where our new insights arise, as well as our ability to nurture and, at its most fundamental level, to create. Our feminine aspect is naturally open, intuitive, creative, and spontaneous. This is why the Inner Author enjoys going with the flow.

When we give our Inner Author permission to come out and play on the page, we find flow and can fill up the blank page in a joyful, even fun way. Flow happens when we slow down our busy mind and tune in to our intuitive guidance as we write, without our Inner Editor breathing down our back.

Understanding how and when to engage our Inner Editor and Inner Author in the process of birthing a book is how our authors achieve the big goal of finishing their first manuscript so swiftly.

Although I've given my Inner Editor a bad rap when it comes to my own experience of writing with flow, we all *need* this part of us to help organize and structure our book's content in a logical way. The Inner Editor plays a vital role in engaging our readers effectively and helping us successfully complete our book. (As do professional editors, which are an absolute must if you want your book to be polished and well received!) It serves us best when we are intentional with assigning our Inner Editor tasks at specific times on our book journey—otherwise, we risk blocking the energy of flow as we write.

As I was writing the first draft of this chapter, I had to chuckle when I caught myself editing as I was typing. A perfect example of how my Inner Editor steps in too soon, stopping my Inner Author from allowing the words to simply flow imperfectly onto the page. I must gently remind my Inner Editor that I won't forget her and let her know that she'll have an important job to do after the first draft is cranked out!

## THE VOICE OF FEAR AND THE VOICE OF LOVE

Okay, I admit I talk to myself a lot. Most of us have inner voices that offer commentary all day long in the background of our minds, whether we're conscious of them or not. These thoughts are either generated by the energy of fear (negativity) or by the energy of love (positivity). These polarized voices within us inform and create our reality, so it's vital to be deliberate in deciding which voice we choose to listen to. Unless we're truly in a life-or-death situation, it will serve us to choose the voice of love: that encouraging and kind inner voice that calls us to step outside of our comfort zone, fueling our vision and growth.

The voice of fear will sabotage us in sneaky ways from moving forward. Remember, this is to keep us safe, to keep us away from change. If we choose to heed the voice of fear and its limiting thoughts and beliefs, we can pretty much guarantee we'll never finish our book. Staying small, staying safe, and staying in our comfort zone is fear's goal. Though writing a book is not a life-threatening commitment, to our fear, it may feel like it is.

Many years ago, I attended my first silent meditation retreat. This was a five-night immersion in the mountains of Colorado not too far from my home, but far enough that it was a welcome escape from my busy life as a mother of young, loud children. I was so looking forward to *silence*. What I didn't know at the time was how loud the voices in my head were—until there I was, immersed day after day in an environment of quiet.

I was camping alone on the 600-acre property in a canvas pup tent set up in the forest. We were asked to set an intention at the beginning of the retreat, and cluelessly, I chose the intention of "releasing *all* of my fears." (If you're a seasoned practitioner, you might be chuckling right now.)

Whenever you want to let go of or release something with intention, you can bet it will come up to be experienced first. So there I was, alone in the pitch-dark wilderness, wind howling night after night, having horrible nightmares of every single one of my biggest fears: losing my children, separation from loved ones, betrayal, annihilation in all manners. Needless to say, I was shaken, humbled, and extremely sleep-deprived.

One afternoon, saddled by exhaustion, I remembered a favorite poem of mine—"The Guest House" by Rumi (2004).

> *This being human is a guest house.*
> *Every morning a new arrival.*
>
> *A joy, a depression, a meanness,*
> *some momentary awareness comes*
> *as an unexpected visitor.*
>
> *Welcome and entertain them all!*
> *Even if they're a crowd of sorrows,*
> *who violently sweep your house*
> *empty of its furniture,*
> *still, treat each guest honorably.*
> *He may be clearing you out*
> *for some new delight.*
>
> *The dark thought, the shame, the malice,*
> *meet them at the door laughing,*
> *and invite them in.*
>
> *Be grateful for whoever comes,*
> *because each has been sent*
> *as a guide from beyond.*

I decided to pull out my journal and host an imaginary tea party on the page. I was inviting every one of my fears to the table. I put out the doormat and welcomed them each in, naming them, pouring imaginary tea, and asking them to tell me whatever they needed to say. I thanked each fear for showing up and wrote down all that they shared.

The next, final morning of the retreat, after another sleepless night of bad dreams, I decided to walk up the mountain trail in the dark to the meditation sanctuary. I was forlorn. My dream of being refreshed and renewed after this five-day silent retreat was laughable. But I couldn't laugh. I was so physically and emotionally exhausted that I felt like a zombie. As I put one foot in front of the other, I could feel nothing except the beating of my heart. I made it to the top of the steep trail just as the first hint of morning light arrived. *I must still be alive*, I thought, as I walked into the empty temple, lit a candle, and sat on a cushion to meditate.

I closed my eyes and began to breathe into my beating heart, the only sensation I could feel. Then I heard the voice of my heart speak to me, gently and lovingly, putting out a welcome mat inviting me and all of my fears inside. In my mind, the doors of my heart looked just like the golden doors of the meditation temple. They opened wide, and one by one, I witnessed each of the fears walking in, followed by myself and my loved ones. In my heart, my fears were transmuted by an all-encompassing unconditional love. I felt deep peace and serenity like nothing I'd felt before.

I share this story because this practice of dialoguing with the voice of fear and the voice of love is how I've been able to "let go" and move through my fears—and it's how my clients have, too. I'll guide you in a practice inspired by this experience at the end of this chapter.

## OPENING TO THE VOICE OF LOVE

The voice and energy of the heart is unconditional love. Love is always more powerful than fear. We have a choice to decide which voice we are going to listen to as we move through our lives—and through big changes like our book-writing journey. But choosing the voice of love takes courage.

The word *courage* comes from the Latin root *cor*, which means "heart." You need courage to take risks; to listen to your heart, your inner wisdom, the voice of your soul; and to trust yourself. When we are brave enough to choose love over fear, we open and unblock our heart chakra so our energy can flow up into the upper chakras, ultimately connecting us to our higher selves and the Universal source of energy beyond.

You have a powerful tool, which you learned in the first step of FLOW: *Follow the breath.* When you slow down and tune in to your inner experience, you'll more easily be able to recognize your subconscious fears and limiting thoughts and beliefs.

By engaging and opening the heart chakra through the suggested practice here, we open the energy of our heart and build a bridge of connection between ourselves and others—including our readers. Fear can block this energy center and keep us disconnected and stuck. But the energy of our heart—and the voice of love—can help us move through and overcome our fear.

> **BOOK BIRTHING TIP**
> **ALCHEMIZE YOUR FEARS**
> Make friends with your fears. Be kind and compassionate. Invite them in and pour them a cup of tea. Listen as they share what they need from you. Shower them with kindness.

Our heart speaks to us with loving-kindness, encouragement, and compassion, knowing that change and transformation are ultimately why we are here in these human bodies. Our souls communicate with us through the heart. The voice of love always encourages us in the direction of growth and transformation.

When you're writing a book, the voice of love may encourage you on with thoughts like . . .

> *You've got this.*
> *Your voice matters.*
> *Your readers are waiting on you to show up for them.*
> *You are courageous.*
> *Writing your book will serve so many who need your wisdom.*

If you don't already hear these kinds of thoughts in your head, practice saying them in your mind. If this is hard for you, imagine this voice as a best friend who has your back and wants you to succeed. Trust these loving words as truth, and let them guide you forward.

## CHAKRA BREATHING PRACTICE

### HEART CHAKRA

I encourage you to record these breathing exercises in your own voice and then play the recording back to yourself, so you can close your eyes and deepen into a guided meditative experience. Find a comfortable seat, propping yourself up on a cushion to make sure that your knees are level with your hips, to avoid unnecessary pressure on your lower spine.

> Close your eyes and begin to tune in to your breath, focusing your awareness on your inhale and your exhale. Follow your breath in through the nostrils, imagining that it's flowing all the way down into your belly. Soften your belly muscles and allow the inhale to fill your pelvic bowl. As you exhale, imagine the breath moving down, out of your body, out of the tailbone or the feet, flowing down into the Earth. Visualize roots extending from your physical body, pushing deep into the Earth, spreading out in all directions, grounding you into the support of the Earth.
>
> Do another round of this inhale through the nose into the belly, and exhale out the body, through the tailbone or feet. This time, on the inhale, breathe light up from the center of the Earth, through all of your roots—up through your root chakra, sacral chakra, and solar plexus chakra—expanding the breath and light into your heart. Notice what's here in your heart space.
>
> As you breathe in, imagine a spiral of energy coming in, a green light illuminating the heart center in the middle of

your chest. Sense any blocks or fears, then exhale the breath out and down through the tailbone or feet, into the Earth. Repeat the cycle of breath, the inhale coming up from the Earth as light flowing into the heart center, spiraling clockwise on the inhale and counterclockwise on the exhale, expanding down out of the body, into the Earth. Breathe this way for several minutes.

When you begin to feel a sense of openness in the center of your chest, imagine breathing in the energy of self-love, self-compassion, and acceptance. Notice whether you feel any resistance or blocks in this energy center, and if you do, continue to use the inhale and exhale to breathe energy from the Earth up into this chakra.

This pattern of breathing will help to clear and balance your heart chakra. When you feel complete, open your eyes and stretch, drink some water, and take a moment to reorient yourself to your environment.

Now is the perfect time to answer the flow-writing prompts that follow.

### HEART CHAKRA FLOW-WRITING PROMPTS

Answer the following questions in your journal. Remember, this is a flow-writing practice. Don't edit—keep your pen moving (or fingers typing) without worrying about grammar or punctuation or whether it's good writing. Set your timer for thirty minutes for this exercise and take longer if you need it.

- Which specific fears are coming up for me on my book-writing journey right now? (For example, fear of failure, fear of success, impostor syndrome, or some other fear.) Write them all down, no matter how small or insignificant they may seem.

- If each fear had a voice, what exactly would it say to me? *Take a moment to deeply listen. Let your words flow and give your fear a voice. Let each fear be heard. When you come to a natural stopping point, pause. Let your fear know you see it and understand it.*
- *Now begin to breathe into your compassionate, unconditionally loving heart chakra. The heart is a great transmuter of our fears.* What would my heart say in response to what my fears have shared? *Again, let your pen flow and the words of your heart pour onto the page.*

When you feel complete, take some time for yourself. Facing your fears is deep work, so you may want to schedule some time alone in nature, in a warm bath, or under the covers for a nap!

# 7
# Own Your Inner Wisdom

*Once we believe in ourselves, we can risk curiosity, wonder, spontaneous delight, or any experience that reveals the human spirit.*

**E. E. CUMMINGS**

**AS YOU BECOME MORE** practiced with discerning, acknowledging, and letting go of limiting beliefs and fears, you are ready for the next step of awakening into FLOW.

You know that encouraging inner voice that has your back? It comes from the heart, and I believe it's the voice of your soul. It's also referred to as our intuitive voice, or Higher Self, guiding us to the right next step on our path, assuring our growth and evolution. We have to get out of our heads to be able to hear it. It may sound like a loving family member or friend, or it may be more of a feeling sense or hunch. It can also show up as a full-body "knowing" (or claircognizance). When we listen to our intuitive voice, we access our inner wisdom. We all have the capacity to tap into the deep well of our inner wisdom, which is a direct path to our personal truth.

When we access our inner wisdom, our writing feels easeful and aligned to our purpose. It's coming through us, and we know it's our truth. To be able to express ourselves this way feels liberating and light. We are in the zone. The flow. And it's possible for all of us to get there.

Our egos help us express our soul's longings. Remember, our ego and our soul are partners! Sometimes the ego's material desires can get in the way. For example, we can get distracted from writing when we imagine stepping into the spotlight as a published book author . . . dreams of fame, sitting on Oprah's couch, or hitting *The New York Times* Best Seller list may carry us away in a rush of excitement about our potential fame, success, or worthiness.

It takes a healthy dose of self-awareness to see that it's okay to have those egoic fantasies and still answer the call of our soul, living into our higher purpose. We can see that by writing our books from a higher perspective, we embody a true servant's heart.

### ENLIGHTEN YOUR READERS WITH YOUR EXPERTISE

Do you have the trifecta of a powerful personal story, expertise in your chosen field, and professional case studies that showcase your success? If so, you have all the ingredients for writing a transformational book that will elevate your credibility and authority.

You will be enlightening your readers to new ways of thinking and seeing, offering your wisdom and expertise as a solution in their lives. If you have professional expertise related to your book's subject matter, *own it*. Be sure to include stories that showcase your experience and the transformation you offer to clients. Recount your client success stories and also your own to inspire your readers. When you include these successes alongside specific themes or points you are trying to make, your readers will begin to see how you can help them, too.

## READ YOUR TESTIMONIALS

Sometimes we're so close to our own work that we forget the powerful transformations and great stories of success of our clients. Helping people who were told they would never bear children to become mothers was a true gift in my holistic fertility practice. When I was writing my first book on that topic and self-doubt started creeping in, I'd go to my website and read the client testimonials. This was a great reminder of *my why* (and you will get clarity about *your why* in Part Three). Reading my clients' praise pulled me out of the impostor spiral and back into my calling to serve through my book.

> **BOOK BIRTHING TIP**
> **BE GRATEFUL**
> Gratitude is a powerful tool for raising your energetic frequency. Remember where you started and how far you've come. Recall the impact you've already made, and be grateful for your work, your health, your home, your loved ones, nourishing food, running water, sunshine, and fresh air.

If you have collected endorsements or positive feedback from your work, read those aloud to yourself! Post the best ones somewhere you'll see them to remind yourself of the impact you've made and to keep you inspired and moving ahead.

## CREATE POSITIVE AFFIRMATIONS

Whether or not you have testimonials, writing and repeating positive affirmations—either silently or out loud—can help to shift negative thought patterns in the brain. Use positive affirmations when you feel stuck and need an uplifting perspective. Every time you repeat these empowering phrases, you create or deepen new neural pathways in the brain that will help to transform your experience.

When you combine positive affirmations with visualization, this dynamic duo can help unblock the flow of energy within the chakras.

The words "I am" are a powerful way to frame an affirmation. Repeating certain sacred sounds and phrases has been an important part of yoga practice since ancient times. These phrases are referred to as mantras. The *Soham* mantra—translated as "I Am That"—is one of the most significant because it connects you to your highest power. (Santos 2020)

For example, if I feel anxious or caught up in worrying thoughts, I might use the following affirmations: *I am grounded. I am safe. I am here.* These all challenge my current frame of mind and help unblock the flow of energy through the root chakra. By using visualization or even physically feeling my feet on the ground, I can imagine sensing the weight of my body supported by the Earth rising up beneath me.

Create an "I am" affirmation that you believe is possible, and visualize feeling that reality in your body. Close your eyes and say the mantra silently or speak it out loud, imagining that it is true. Acting "as if" something is already a reality raises your energetic frequency to match and attract that reality.

Choose a word or phrase that resonates with you to shift into a more positive and aligned energetic state. Do this while visualizing yourself feeling the reality of that phrase.

Here are some effective affirmations for unblocking the energy flow of each chakra . . .

> **Root Chakra**—I am here and grounded.
> **Sacral Chakra**—I am inspired and creative.

**Solar Plexus Chakra**—I am confident and committed to my goals.
**Heart Chakra**—I am compassionate and loving.
**Throat Chakra**—I am a clear communicator who speaks my truth.
**Third Eye Chakra**—I am intuitive and wise.
**Crown Chakra**—I am a channel for Divine creative energy to flow through.

The soul needs the ego to fulfill its mission! We need the soul and ego to become partners in this dance of writing a book and then stepping into the spotlight with our wisdom and expertise.

This is where the upper chakras support us. They are a direct line from our ego to our soul, or to the Universe, God, Spirit, or whatever you may call that force beyond that's bigger than your ego or its drive.

> **BOOK BIRTHING TIP**
> **AFFIRM YOUR AWESOMENESS**
> Write down the affirmations that resonate with you on slips of paper. Add them to your altar or tape them up where you'll see them regularly. Rewire the inner voice of fear with these encouraging statements.

How do we become the channel for our deepest knowing, our inner wisdom, to flow through us onto the page?

We trust. We listen deeply. We let go of outer distractions. And then we awaken into flow.

### THROAT CHAKRA BREATHING: CLARIFY YOUR VOICE

Speaking words of affirmation aloud is a powerful practice. When we're able to speak (and write) our authentic truth, we are accessing the energy of the heart chakra and expressing ourselves from a place of sovereignty and self-compassion.

Record the following breathing practices in your own voice and play each one back, so you can deepen into the experience as a guided practice. I invite you to do just one chakra breathing practice and flow-writing practice at a time to fully digest the experience of each chakra.

**CHAKRA BREATHING PRACTICE**

**THROAT CHAKRA**

Close your eyes and begin to tune in to your inhale and your exhale. Follow your breath in through the nostrils, all the way down into your belly. Soften your belly muscles and allow the inhale to fill your pelvic bowl. As you exhale, imagine the breath moving down out of your body, out of the tailbone or the feet, flowing down into the Earth. Visualize roots extending down from your physical body deep into the Earth, spreading out in all directions, grounding you in the support of the Earth.

Do another round of this—inhale through the nose, into the belly, and exhale out the body, through the tailbone or feet. This time, on the inhale, breathe light up from the center of the Earth, through your roots, up through your root chakra, sacral chakra, solar plexus chakra, and heart chakra. Keep drawing the light up through your body, expanding the breath, and breathe the light up into your throat.

As you breathe in, imagine a spiral of energy coming in, a blue light illuminating the throat chakra. Sense any restrictions or tightness, and allow the warmth of your breath to melt tension out with the exhale. Send the breath down, through the tailbone or feet, into the Earth. Repeat the cycle of breath, the inhale coming up from the Earth as light flows into the throat, spiraling clockwise on the inhale and counterclockwise on the exhale, expanding down, out of the body, into the

Earth. You may want to sigh audibly or allow any other sounds to flow out with the breath. Breathe this way for several minutes.

Imagine breathing the energy of the heart up into the throat, bathing this center in self-love, self-compassion, and acceptance. Notice whether you feel any resistance or blocks in your throat chakra, and if you do, you may want to use the vocal cords on the exhale in whatever way feels good. Sometimes this can sound like sighing, singing a tone, or just exhaling with a growl or hum.

This pattern of breathing will help to clear and balance your throat chakra. When you feel complete, open your eyes, and stretch, drink some water, and take a moment to reorient yourself to your environment.

---

**THROAT CHAKRA FLOW-WRITING PROMPTS**

Set a timer for five minutes per question and start writing, keeping your pen moving (or your fingers typing) until the timer is done. Let go of editing, or worrying about grammar, punctuation, or spelling. Just allow whatever words that come to come. Trust your Inner Author to simply flow.

- Do I have any hesitations about sharing my voice? My story? Or about speaking my truth?
- If so, what fears are coming up for me about speaking my truth?
- How do I feel about stepping into my role as an authority and expert voice on the topic of my book?
- What might be holding me back from claiming my expertise on my topic?
- What kind of feedback or praise do I have that might prove I'm qualified to write this book?

## CHAKRA BREATHING PRACTICE

### THIRD EYE

Close your eyes and begin to tune in to your inhale and your exhale. Follow your breath in through the nostrils all the way down into your belly. Soften your belly muscles and allow the inhale to fill your pelvic bowl. As you exhale, imagine the breath moving down, out of your body, out of the tailbone or the feet, flowing down into the Earth. Visualize roots extending from your physical body deep into the Earth, spreading out in all directions, grounding you into the support of the Earth.

Do another round of this inhale through the nose into the belly, and exhale out the body through the tailbone or feet. This time on the inhale, breathe light up from the center of the Earth, through your roots, up through your root chakra, sacral chakra, solar plexus, heart, and throat, and expanding the breath and light up into your third eye.

As you breathe in, imagine a spiral of energy coming into the third eye, an indigo color that illuminates the third eye chakra between the brows. Sense any restrictions or tightness, and allow the warmth of your breath to melt tension out with the exhale. Send the breath down through the tailbone or feet into the Earth. Repeat the cycle of breath, the inhale coming up from the Earth as light flowing into the third eye, spiraling clockwise on the inhale and counterclockwise on the exhale, expanding down out of the body into the Earth. Breathe this way for a couple of minutes.

As you tune in to the third eye, you begin to awaken your intuition and inner wisdom. Imagine yourself on a path in the woods. Ahead of you on the trail, you see a person walking toward you with smiling eyes and an open heart. As they approach you, you feel their energy of love and excitement expanding toward you.

As they get closer, you realize this person is an older, wiser version of yourself. This is your Inner Wise One, the one who has already written the book. The one who has overcome obstacles and is beckoning you forward on your path. Their eyes are beaming love toward you. You feel safe, seen, and supported by this being. You feel inspired to ask this wise self about whatever has been holding you back.

Ask them, "What do I need to know right now?" Breathe and listen for an answer for several minutes . . . whether you receive a direct answer or not, trust that the answer will come in its own time. You may thank this Wise One for meeting you here in whatever way feels most comfortable—a bow, a hug, a handshake—knowing that you can come back here at any time.

Return to your body, breathing into the third eye and exhaling down into the Earth. When you feel grounded and present, open your eyes and stretch, drink some water, and take a moment to reorient yourself into your environment.

Now is the perfect time to answer the flow-writing prompts that follow.

---

### THIRD EYE FLOW-WRITING PROMPTS

Set your timer for fifteen minutes and answer the following prompts, keeping your pen moving or your fingers typing, and letting the words flow onto the page.

- What did my Inner Wise One look like?
- What did I ask them?

- What (if any) intuitive guidance did I receive from them?
- How did I feel in their presence?
- What insights or intuitive guidance about my book have I received prior to this experience? Have I followed it? Why or why not?

## CHAKRA BREATHING PRACTICE

### CROWN CHAKRA

Close your eyes and begin to tune in to your breath. Bring your awareness to your inhale and your exhale. Follow your breath in through the nostrils, all the way down into your belly. Soften your belly muscles and allow the inhale to fill your pelvic bowl. As you exhale, imagine the breath moving down out of your body, out of the tailbone or the feet, flowing down into the Earth. Visualize roots extending down from your physical body, deep into the Earth, spreading out in all directions, grounding you in the support of the Earth.

Inhale again through the nose into the belly, and exhale out the body, through the tailbone or feet. On your next inhale, breathe clear light up from the center of the Earth, through your roots up through all of your chakras to the top of your skull. Imagine the light filling your entire head, then visualize breathing it back down into the Earth.

As you breathe in again, imagine a spiral of energy coming in, moving to the top of the head, a violet light illuminating and opening the crown chakra. See this light extending out the top of your head and opening to the Universal energy above and beyond your physical self. Sense any restrictions here, and allow the warmth of your breath to melt tension out with the exhale. Inhale the breath up and out the top of the head, and then imagine it flowing back down with the exhale, through the tailbone or feet, into the Earth. Repeat the cycle of breath, the inhale coming up from the Earth as light flowing into the top of the head, spiraling clockwise on the inhale and counterclockwise on the exhale, then expanding down, out of the body, into the Earth. Breathe this way for several minutes.

If you sense any blocks in your crown chakra, imagine breathing the energy of the heart up into the head, circulating self-love, self-compassion, and acceptance through the brain and skull.

This pattern of breathing will help to clear and balance your crown chakra, so you can connect with the Universal source of energy beyond your physical self. When you feel complete, open your eyes and stretch, drink some water, and take a moment to reorient yourself to your environment.

### CROWN CHAKRA FLOW-WRITING PROMPTS

- What are some things I've recently manifested that have proven I have the power to create my own reality?
- How do I describe and connect with a "higher" or Universal energy source outside of myself? *(You may call it the Universe, God, Source, Spirit, Higher Self, nature, or something else.)*
- How do I intentionally nurture this connection?
- How might I be more intentional to open to this higher wisdom?

These practices will help you transcend the egoic conditioning and fear that can limit you, helping you gain a greater understanding and trust in your intuitive voice and inner wisdom.

The upper three chakras in the physical body help us access our higher selves, where we discover our personal truth and connect to a source of higher intelligence. With practice and self-awareness, we can bring our breath and intention to these energy centers, seeing our patterns more clearly and supporting the balance and flow of energy through us, so we can finally understand what it means to awaken into flow and write from the heart.

# 8

# Write From the Heart

*Our creative dreams and yearnings come from a divine source.
As we move toward our dreams, we move toward our divinity.*

JULIA CAMERON, FROM *THE ARTIST'S WAY*

**WHAT DOES IT MEAN** to write from the heart?

To write from the heart is to have the courage and to trust ourselves enough to be authentic and vulnerable as we write: allowing our intuitive guidance, aka our Inner Author, to play on the page.

As you learned in Chapter 4, the heart chakra is the fourth chakra in the body, sitting between the three lower chakras and the three upper chakras. It is the bridge connecting our egoic selves to our higher selves. The heart chakra is the energy center that activates the voice of love. From our heart, we can express our voice with the energy of love, empathy, and compassion. The voice of the heart is the natural antidote to the voice of fear.

To write with flow, we must let go of overthinking and perfectionism. When we follow the breath, we drop out of our busy minds and into our hearts, letting go of fear and embracing our inner wisdom.

The Inner Author thrives in flow and is associated with the right side of your brain—your intuitive, feeling self. Your Inner Author lives in the present moment, not in the future and not in the past. To get into the present moment and a state of flow with your writing, and to awaken your brilliant Inner Author, you must activate your heart chakra energy. This is how you *write from the heart*.

I bet you feel what I mean here intuitively, because you lead with your heart! You are being called to serve through your words. With more and more AI-generated content out there in the world, readers seeking transformation crave real, heart-led voices. When you write from the heart, you have the power to connect, inspire, transform, and elevate lives with your words.

When you understand the power of writing from the heart, it's easier to get out of your own way and let your writing be divinely guided. When you balance your intellect with your intuition and your mind with your heart, you are primed to write words that engage your readers and attract them to you.

The heart chakra is our energetic portal of compassion and connection. Through the heart, we relate more deeply with the world. We all have access to this energy within us. When we write from the heart, we tap into a well of creativity and authenticity that shines on the page and magnetizes those who are meant to find us.

Writing from the heart comes from a desire to connect deeply with your readers. To write from the heart takes intention and courage. In one of its earliest forms, the word *courage* meant "to speak one's mind by telling all one's heart." You must embrace vulnerability and open your heart to your readers. Your empathy for your readers helps your words reach in and touch their longings and desires. Chapter by chapter, they feel seen by you. Page by page, they deepen their trust in you. When your reader feels this way due to your own vulnerability and can empathize with your experience, you become relatable and trustworthy. Your reader will sense your heart, which will support the intimate connection you're building with them.

## USING YOUR SENSES

As humans, we have access to a range of emotions that we can express through our voice and tone in our writing—something computer-generated content just can't do. The range of feelings we experience allows us to process our world through our senses. When we skillfully use our senses in our writing, our readers feel as if we're sitting across the table from them.

Our nervous systems are designed to connect us with our environment—seeing, hearing, touching, smelling, and tasting all that is around us. This connection through our senses is what makes being human so interesting, and it's also part of what makes great writing. When we use the senses to "paint a scene" for our readers, they are transported with us and feel our words more easily and deeply.

For example, as I type this sentence, I have been occasionally glancing over my computer monitor through the tall windows of my home office, into a forest of evergreens freshly blanketed in snow. Nature is my muse, and I am forever grateful to live in the mountains of Colorado, where I can step into the wilderness right outside of my door to get inspiration.

> **BOOK BIRTHING TIP**
>
> **TAKE NATURE BREAKS**
>
> Get outside. Follow your breath. Open your senses to see the natural beauty. Feel the air on your skin. Let the sounds of nature boost your energy: birdsong, a flowing stream, wind in the trees. Nature balances and aligns our chakras. Sit at the base of a tree, feel your roots, and enjoy!

Though it's below freezing outside as I write today, I'm warm and cozy inside, wearing a sweater and slippers, sitting at my desk, sipping a comforting mug of herbal chai, as I witness the slow melt happening just beyond my office in the afternoon sun. The golden light is warming up the frosty boughs, icicles are glistening on the tips of pine needles, silver crystals of water shimmer and drip, as out-of-sight branches shed the weight of melting snow. White drifts cascade by, catching my attention and drawing my eyes past the panes. My supportive partner gently taps on the door to deliver a steaming bowl of rice and vegetable curry to my desk, a much-appreciated fuel for my writing.

Every one of our senses has the potential to bring us into the present moment and open our heart. Our sense of sight may open the portal to our heart when we see our beloved looking deeply into our eyes with tender care. Our sense of hearing may connect us to something outside of ourselves, such as birdsong or a gently trickling stream. Cozy as I am here in my office, I can feel a sense of warmth and comfort creating a safe container for me to open and write without editing—a welcome practice I've developed after years of retraining my Inner Editor.

Oh, I can still hear her voice, like a whiny kid in the back seat repeatedly asking "Are we there yet?" She's tapping me on the shoulder, wondering if the scene I just painted was good enough. Did it convey what I was trying to convey? Will my readers be pulled in as I intended?

Guess what? I don't have to answer her right now. I get to keep on driving forward, allowing my Inner Author to flow. She's the one who just gets to let the words out of my head, through my typing fingers, onto the page.

It's a practice. I know I'll have time to come back and reread my writing later, after I get through the first draft of my manuscript, and then I can give my Inner Editor free rein. She used to be a lot louder, trust me. She's learning that her time will come, so now she's napping in the back seat as my Inner Author fills up the page with words. And not just any words. Words that matter for you at this stage of our journey together, dear reader. I want to give you permission to just let the words flow out of you—uncensored, unedited, and raw.

If you know Julia Cameron's writing, you may be familiar with the "morning pages" practice she presents in her highly successful book *The Artist's Way* (2016). It's a practice to help us get into a daily habit of waking up and "purging out" three pages of whatever is top of mind, to clear out the cobwebs.

I am a firm believer in journaling, as you know by now. The point of writing without censoring—without fear, without self-doubt, without constant editing—is to set your Inner Author free!

So many great books that could serve humanity are trapped inside the brains of aspiring authors whose Inner Editors keep them stuck. This is a real shame!

## FINDING YOUR VOICE

Knowing who your Ideal Reader is, inside and out, is gold when it comes time to write. Imagine your reader sitting across from you, sharing a drink or a meal or perhaps a cup of tea. How would you speak to them about the idea you're trying to write about?

*Write it just like you would say it.*

This means you must understand your Ideal Reader well enough to meet them exactly where they are. (You'll get a chance to explore your Ideal Reader more in Part Three.) You likely know how great it feels to be seen by someone who "gets you". That is how you want your readers to feel.

You may be uncertain of how to really connect with your readers on the page. But trust me: Let down your guard, even just a teeny bit, and show your humanity. Do this by imagining your Ideal Reader struggling with the problem you can help them solve, and your heart will open. And from that place, you can write with genuine empathy and understanding, as if you were face-to-face in a heartfelt conversation. That's how they will feel seen by you. They will immediately sense that you "get" them. They will begin to trust that you can lead them to their desired outcome.

When I was thinking about you (yes, you are *my* Ideal Reader!), I decided to choose the voice and tone of a close friend or trusted guide. You may want to choose the tone of a coach, someone who builds up and inspires, or even someone who has a tough-love or humorous approach. Or maybe you will choose more of an "expert" tone and write in the conversational tone you might take in your office with a client. Whatever voice you choose, be YOU and be consistent, and remember that you want your reader to trust you and relate to you.

## VULNERABILITY AND TRUST

When your readers see you as a source they can trust, they will begin to see how you can help them solve their problem. Perhaps you've been through your own challenge and solved a problem similar to theirs, like when I was stuck writing my first book but then figured out how to achieve my dream.

I never would have imagined that I would publish a book, achieve a bonus bestseller in the book's top category, then go on to win two book awards and coach dozens of others in achieving their book-publishing dreams.

Maybe you've overcome a hurdle, found deep insight, or learned the hard way how to accomplish a goal. And you're reading this book to help others accomplish what you've accomplished.

To build trust, you must let your readers in, share your own human challenges, and connect with them about the trials and errors that you have endured. Nobody is perfect, and believe me, your readers will trust you even more if you can admit your own struggles. The more vulnerable you are about your own story of transformation, the more relatable you become to your reader, and the more you can help them feel that they aren't alone in their journey. With your support, your readers can begin to think, *Well, if they experienced these challenges and fears and found a way through, then maybe I can, too.*

Which brings me back to the topic of fear. As we share our stories with our readers, including our fears, vulnerabilities, failures, and successes, we invoke a sense of compassion in those witnessing our journey. Understanding our own fears helps us have compassion for our readers, too. We can see their pain and suffering, and we want to help by sharing the wisdom we've gained and the resources that have helped us

> **BOOK BIRTHING TIP**
>
> **OPEN YOUR HEART**
>
> If you have an exercise ball, lie on your back over the ball and allow your body to open up in a backbend. Breathe into your heart, sensing the energy flowing. If you don't have an exercise ball, simply clasp your hands behind your back and breathe into your heart. Drop your shoulders. Feel your chest muscles stretching, visualizing your heart chakra energy flowing with each inhale and exhale.

on our own path. We can help our readers face their own fears. And when we have developed, through our own life experience, a tried-and-true solution to a problem, we can be of great service to a much broader range of people through our book.

When you're inspired to serve and support your readers—rather than simply focusing on the book as a means to establish your authority, build your brand, or triple your income (even though those things may happen)—you become much more genuine and trustworthy. In turn, your ideal readers will be more likely to seek out your support beyond the book.

## WORDS ARE ENERGY

Remember that your words have the power to either magnetize or repel. Your energy is palpable through your words and your writing. We all experience a range of energy throughout each day, based on our emotions. From highs to lows.

You can alter your energetic frequency or vibration simply by changing how you feel. When you raise your energetic frequency, your writing becomes more engaging and magnetic. A tool I created called the Writer Frequency Scale will help you assess your energetic frequency so you know where you are on the scale when you sit down to write.

This is an invaluable tool I share with every single author I coach. The scale and the high-vibe practices that follow will help you assess, evaluate, and elevate your energy *before* you sit down to write. Why does this matter? Because if you're feeling agitated or uninspired, that is not a time to work on your book.

This scale along with the high-vibe practices will help you dig yourself out of a low mood and move up in energetic frequency, so that you can write from a place of flow and inspiration.

## WRITER FREQUENCY SCALE

| −10 to −6 | −5 to 0 | +1 to +4 | +5 to +7 | +8 to +10 |
|---|---|---|---|---|
| Completely blocked, bad mood, disconnected from *your why*, stuck in mental melodrama | Feeling low energy, resisting, distracting yourself, procrastinating | Feeling ready to write; committed to sitting down, but not feeling that inspired | Feeling inspired, clear about your goal, ready to meet that word count | Feeling in the flow, connected, buzzing with positive energy, ready to serve, could write for hours |

### BEFORE YOU WRITE

- Know where you are on the scale.

- Engage in your choice of high-vibe practices to move you up the scale. (See the following page.)

- Be compassionate toward yourself when you find yourself at zero or a negative number on the scale. Take a break and reorganize your closet for fifteen minutes if that's all you're inspired to do . . . and then try a high-vibe practice to move you up the scale.

- If you are at +1 to +4, keep adding on high-vibe practices until inspiration strikes, then write, write, write!

## HIGH-VIBE PRACTICES: IDEAS TO RAISE YOUR WRITER VIBE AND GET INTO THE STATE OF FLOW

**Strike a pose!** Try a confidence-boosting "power pose" like Superman or Wonder Woman—put your hands on your hips or stretch your arms out above, reaching for the stars. These postures make you feel physically powerful, cueing the mind to overcome self-doubt, impostor syndrome, or other self-defeating mind games.

**Make a high-vibe playlist!** Create a playlist of uplifting songs for your dancing/singing pleasure. Choose songs with positive, motivating lyrics to boost your mindset and lift your energy.

**Dance, dance, dance!** Whether it's to your high-vibe playlist or another favorite song, move your body to get your blood pumping and release any mental funk. This can be done anywhere, but kitchen floors tend to make great dance floors.

**Step away from your computer!** Go outside, soak up some sunshine on your front porch, or hit a nearby trail for some back-to-nature therapy. Our chakras rebalance and recalibrate in nature, so practice being mindful, tuning in to your senses, soaking up the natural beauty, and remembering to pay atttention to your breath. Fresh air refreshes the brain, too!

**Sweat!** Sometimes dancing is enough, but other times, you may need a high-intensity workout to sweat out your stuckness. Try a trail run or bike ride to get all the benefits of nature, or go to a class at the gym that will get your heart racing.

**Tap!** Just a few minutes of tapping (or acupressure) can wake up the brain by activating energy flow in the meridians on the head. Begin by gently stretching or massaging the neck and shoulders to relieve muscular tension. Using the pads of your fingers on each hand, tap along the jawline on both sides of the face from the ears to the chin and back. Remember to breathe as you tap! Tap on either side of the nose over the sinuses and follow the cheekbones out to the ears. Tap over the temples and forehead, and tap on the third eye to wake up your intuition. Tap up over the top of the head, down the back of the head, along the base of the cranium and back up the sides of the head to the crown. Repeat as desired.

**Nourish!** Make sure you are well-hydrated and eating high-protein meals every three to four hours to optimize your brain function. Sleep is vital, too. For the best brain-boosting power, get seven to eight hours of uninterrupted sleep each night.

(See Thank You & Additional Resources section in the back for a downloadable Writer Frequency Scale and High-Vibe Practices to keep handy as you write.)

## COMING BACK INTO THE MOMENT

As mentioned, the word *inspiration* is derived from the word *inspire*, which means "to breathe" in Latin. Yep, we're back to breathing again. Following the breath—each inhale and exhale—is the first step of FLOW. This handy tool for bringing yourself into the present moment is also a powerful way to increase inspiration and move your energy up the scale, toward a higher frequency.

At the beginning of this chapter, I described the scene of the afternoon sun melting the snow outside my window. Hopefully, my writing conveyed the inspiration I felt in that moment. Now it's dusk, the light has faded, the temperature outside has dropped, and new layers of ice are crystalizing on the branches and trees. I realize I've been sitting here for a couple of hours now and need a break.

I suggest more frequent breaks than every two hours. Yet sometimes when you're in the flow, you lose track of time, and that's okay. Just pay attention to your energy level to cue yourself that a break might be needed.

I get up and stretch, pet my dog, get a snack and a glass of water. I feel that my energy is waning. It's time to wind down for the evening. But if I want to bang out the rest of this chapter, I will need to raise my energy. I have some choices. I can play an inspiring song; I can do some qigong or get up and dance; I can take a short walk before it's totally dark outside. All of these things will reset my energy and impact where I land on the Writer Frequency Scale. Currently, I'm at about a 3.

> **BOOK BIRTHING TIP**
> **MOVE YOUR BODY**
> Sitting at the computer for long stretches of time can block the magic of flow. Set a timer for intentional breaks. Get up, stretch, and drink a full glass of water. Dance, shake, do some gentle yoga or qigong. Get out of your head and wake up the energy in your body.

I choose the walk. It is refreshing to move my body up the mountain road and arrive at the frozen creek, where a hole in the ice broadcasts the gurgling sounds of the running water below. Ah, flow. Nature always shows me what I need in the moment. I listen deeply as the darkness envelops me, tuning in to the moment—the cleansing sound of the mountainside creek, the cold, fresh mountain air filling my lungs. My feet, warm in snow boots, resting on the Earth, feeling her support beneath me. Not thinking about this chapter or what I might write next. Just pure presence.

And that, my friend, is available to all of us. Come back to the senses and into the moment. When you take a short break, it's like hitting refresh on your browser. If it's a longer break, it's like restarting the computer when the pinwheel keeps spinning. Everything works better when rebooted. Give yourself permission for a pause or reset.

Which is what I do next when I call it a wrap for the day. Twenty-five hundred words down, and I've got the bones of Chapter 7 of the book. Not perfect, but it doesn't have to be. My Inner Author got to do what she was born to do. And my Inner Editor . . . well, she'll have her time to make sense of it all three chapters from now, when I'm officially done writing my first rough draft.

**CHAKRA BREATHING PRACTICE**

**ROOT TO CROWN, BECOMING THE TREE**

I encourage you to record these breathing exercises in your own voice and then play the recording back to yourself, so you can close your eyes and deepen into a guided meditative experience. This is a standing meditation, and if you can do this guided practice outside in the presence of a large tree, even better.

> Feel your feet connecting to the Earth, aligning your ankles, knees, hips, and shoulders in the same vertical plane. Feel your spine extending up and your head elongating from the neck to the crown, pulling your chin back so your ears are directly above the shoulders. Close your eyes and begin to tune in to your inner experience by focusing on your inhale and your exhale. Follow your breath in through the nostrils, imagining it flowing all the way down into your belly. Soften your abdominal muscles and allow the breath to come down into your pelvic bowl.
>
> As you exhale, imagine the breath moving out of your feet, flowing down into the Earth. Visualize roots extending from your feet deep into the Earth's center.
>
> Do another round of this—inhale through the nose, into the belly, and exhale out the body through the feet, deep into the Earth's core. On your next inhale, breathe clear light up from

the center of the Earth and into your physical body through your feet. Keep breathing this white light up through each chakra, from the root to the sacral, solar plexus, heart, throat, third eye, and crown chakras. See the column of light moving out the top of your head, connecting with the Universal energy source above.

Then, as you breathe out, imagine the clear light from above coming back down through the chakras, moving through the crown, third eye, throat, heart, solar plexus, sacral, and root chakras, out the feet, extending deep into the center of the Earth. Be like a tree: Sense your roots grounding you, anchoring you in the support of the Earth, and feel your torso extending up, like a tall trunk reaching up to the sky.

Repeat this inhale and exhale cycle again, opening up to the energy of the Earth below and the Universe above. Become the channel between the Earth and the Universe, the ego and the soul.

This pattern of breathing will help to open you up to Divine inspiration and Universal wisdom, while keeping you rooted and grounded in your body. When you feel complete, open your eyes and stretch, drink some water, and take a moment to reorient yourself to your environment.

Now is the perfect time to answer the flow-writing prompts that follow.

---

### FLOW-WRITING PROMPTS

Set a timer for five minutes per question and start writing, keeping your pen moving (or your fingers typing) until the timer is done. Let go of editing or worrying about grammar, punctuation, or spelling. Trust your Inner Author to simply flow.

- Do I resist being vulnerable about my own story as I write to my readers? Why or why not?
- How can I empathize with the struggle my readers might be experiencing?
- How can I help my readers feel seen?

As we come to the close of the FLOW Method section of this book, I encourage you to pause here and digest all that you've experienced in this process of looking within. When you are willing to do the FLOW Method practices and embrace your own personal journey of growth, you are moving much closer to joining that 3 percent of aspiring authors who actually publish their books.

Why? When you can see your own internal blocks and limitations as an underlying source of what's keeping you stuck, you can eliminate most of the struggle and unnecessary delays in your book-birthing journey. But these practices take practice! I highly recommend you come back to them as you are writing your book's chapters to overcome obstacles, elevate your energy, and awaken into flow.

# PART THREE

# The Way Forward

# 9
# Know Your Why

*Energy is the essence of life. Every day you decide how you're going to use it by knowing what you want and what it takes to reach that goal, and by maintaining focus.*

**OPRAH WINFREY**

**HOPEFULLY, BY NOW YOU** have engaged the practices and flow-writing prompts in Part Two of the book to help bring more clarity, insight, and flow into your experience of writing. Having an experiential awareness of your energy and how to overcome internal obstacles will ensure your success in this next part.

With tools on hand for the inner journey of writing a book, it's time to roll up your sleeves and build a solid foundation for its structure. Mapping out the content and organizing your chapters begins with an important and often-overlooked first step: your vision.

You may feel pulled to write your book, but do you know exactly why?

Before you build a house, you start with a strong foundation, right? The same goes for crafting your book. Before you begin to build your outline, you need a solid foundation, which comes from understanding your vision and goals, aka *your why*.

## CRYSTALIZING YOUR VISION

Without a clear understanding of *your why* and a clear focus on your destination, the book-writing trip will easily meander, zigzag, lose direction, and have a much higher chance of slowly petering out. If you want to succeed in finishing your book and getting it into the world, the most important foundational step is to get laser-focused on where you want to end up. When you have the clarity of your destination in mind, you can relax and enjoy the journey, trusting your inner wisdom and your Inner Author to be your guides.

There may be a few different reasons you feel called to write a book. Maybe you love to write and have dreamed about becoming an author since you were young. Or maybe you don't (yet) love to write but have a transformational process or framework you know can help others. Perhaps you want to become known as a thought leader in your field, sharing your passion for your subject matter, and you know that becoming a published author will help you build a platform to expand your reach and impact.

If you have the desire to write a transformational book that will positively impact your readers' lives (the book you see in your visualizations), then without a doubt, the world needs your book, and your readers are depending on you to follow through and finish it!

## BEGIN WITH YOUR INTUITION

Have you done the short visualization activity from Chapter 1 yet? If not, I encourage you to do so now. When you take time to go within, imagine your book in your mind, and listen to your intuitive guidance, you gain much clarity about your path.

It makes the book-writing process so much easier when you thoughtfully consider what your success will look like *after* you've written the book and it's in your readers' hands.

Equally important to *your why* is *your how*—how you envision your book elevating your authority and subject-matter expertise. How will writing a successful book help you achieve your vision? Will your readers ideally become clients? Will you line up paid speaking events? Will you fill up a program or retreat you're offering? It's so important to understand the details of your specific goals: they will help inform and shape the content you'll include in your book.

### MEMOIR OR TRANSFORMATIONAL NONFICTION?

Our accomplished client Bobbi came to us with a draft of her memoir. She had lived through a terrible tragedy decades before that led her down a new career path of supporting others as they navigated violent trauma. Through her own healing process, she studied with pioneers in the field of trauma, obtained her PhD, and eventually launched her private practice focused on workplace well-being.

She was a gifted writer with a compelling story to tell, which is why her friends encouraged her to write a memoir. However, she left out how she had taken that personal tragedy and turned it into a career supporting others, for which she had countless case studies and inspirational stories showcasing her success with clients. Through our coaching, she realized she had started writing her memoir without clarity about her goals for how the book might serve her business and help attract new clients. We worked together to identify her goals, align the content with her Ideal Reader, and include tools to help them on their journey. She also added several client stories that would show readers how she could possibly help them, too.

Another author of ours Nicole also came to us with a smartly written draft of her memoir. She was a psychotherapist with an ample list of clients, but she wanted to scale up her practice, bring on other therapists, and have someone else run it so she could launch a speaking career—her real passion. She knew she had a compelling and useful story, so she'd been working with a book editor who helped her shape the storyline and ensure the writing was engaging. And it was! However, she was second-guessing her *why* and wasn't sure a memoir would help with her long-term vision or business goals.

With our support, Nicole took the bones of her memoir and envisioned how she could turn parts of her story into specific talks aimed at helping build her speaking career. She then added professional case studies to illustrate her points and increase her perceived authority on the subject matter. The result was a best-selling book that led to a podcast and a growing speaking career, while her practice continues to thrive under new management to free up her time.

Writing a manuscript *before* you know how your book will serve your ultimate goals is a classic example of putting the cart before the horse. I've seen too many authors do this. They have expertise that can benefit many people who would be interested in their professional services and offerings, but they're not clear on the format necessary to get their message out in the most effective way.

When you know *your why* and your goals as an author, you better understand the content you must include in your book to help you achieve them.

## POSITIONING YOURSELF AS AN EXPERT

Organizing your book's material around your professional expertise will help you position yourself as a sought-after speaker. Published authors are often seen as authorities on their subject matter and are invited more frequently to be guest speakers by organizations concerned with similar issues. Whether they're on podcasts, webinars, stages, or conferences, a published author has the potential to charge significantly more than other speakers because their book positions them as a sought-after subject-matter expert. Being a published author elevates your credibility and opens doors, helping readers to know and trust you—and want more of what you have to offer.

## WHAT ARE YOUR REVENUE GOALS?

Once you understand how your book can help serve your audience, it's important to determine your specific revenue goals.

Let's say you're a healer, coach, or consultant who desires more clients. Do you know what rates you'll charge or how many new clients you need per month to meet your revenue goal? Or perhaps you're launching a program, workshop, or retreat, and you want to make a 50 percent profit. Do you know your up-front costs and how many people you'll need to enroll to meet your profit goal? If you dream of pivoting into a speaking career, do you know who you'll pitch for your talk and what fees you'll charge?

Getting specific and crunching your numbers will inspire your forward momentum and help motivate you to move toward your dreams.

Our brains need concrete reasons to keep pushing forward! And for most of us who live under the thumb of capitalism, an increase in income is a carrot to dangle over that first-draft finish line!

## BRANDING YOURSELF AS AN AUTHOR

How you communicate your message to those you want to attract is critical. Some call this marketing or even branding.

If you're a coach or consultant, you're representing the brand of your business, or maybe your method/message/platform is the brand, especially if you're a leader who is passionate about a certain topic.

When you become a published author, you will instantly be seen as an authority on your book's subject matter, and then you will become the brand, which you'll need to promote if you want to align with your vision and meet your goals. Any author who wants to sell books or expand their reach must put on the marketing and sales hat at some point if they want to be successful.

When I was struggling to write my first book, I dug deep to look at the underlying fears fueling my resistance. Memories of earlier public speaking nightmares popped up, where I froze on stage and forgot everything I was supposed to say. Authors have to be public-facing, talking about their book, and my fear of public speaking was holding me back from finishing my book; my resistance was protecting me from having to promote myself and experience public humiliation again. I didn't want to be a brand that I needed to market! Frankly I still don't love it, but I know that if I want to serve those who can benefit from my book, I must be visible and willing to speak about my subject-matter expertise.

My reasons were legit from fear's perspective: I was afraid to be seen. Not just the innate fear that's wired into us when we step outside our comfort zone, but terrified as in freeze-on-stage wordless. I dreaded experiencing that again. I didn't consciously think this when I was struggling with this resistance, but I knew it must've been buried deep within: *Please, just let me hide behind the words of my book, thank you very much.*

The more I explored my fears and limiting beliefs by faithfully using the practices I'm offering in this book, the more I saw how my resistance was actually selfish: I was going to withhold life-changing information that my readers needed to ease their suffering—all because of stage fright?

> **BOOK BIRTHING TIP**
>
> **BE OF SERVICE**
>
> When you can see your book as an act of service for your readers, you cultivate the courage to step up and shine!

This insight helped me see that my calling wasn't about *me*: my goal was to help make a positive impact on my readers' lives. Not finishing my book was simply a way to protect my wounded, fearful ego. Writing and selling my book (which meant selling myself as the author, too) was in service of those I believed could benefit from my knowledge. *Owning my inner wisdom* and sharing my expertise with more people could help others whom I couldn't reach without having a book. Bingo.

Once I understood this, I could see the way forward and stay focused on getting my book done.

## CHOOSING THE RIGHT FOCUS

As you begin to clarify your vision and see how your book can support your goals, you will be better equipped to organize its content to serve those goals.

For example, if you want more clients, you might organize your book's material around how your work has helped current clients and how it will support future ones. If you want your book to help build your speaking career, what are the specific topics you want to speak about? Are there certain types of audiences you envision speaking to? What type of event or platform will help you reach those people?

This is how you decide which content matters most to present in your book.

Like many first-time authors, you likely have a lot of ideas swirling in your head for what to include in your book. When you understand your vision for how your book can serve your goals, you may discover that you have multiple books in you, not just one. Or maybe there's a way to weave the different threads together in one great first book written in service of your goals and readers. This is why knowing your goals matters. Once you do, you can tap into your intuition and inner wisdom through meditation and visualization to access more clarity.

## DRILLING DOWN YOUR WHY

To clarify *your why*, you must start by answering three important questions:

1. What is the outcome you wish for your book's readers?
2. What action(s) do you want them to take after reading your book?
3. How do you envision your book supporting you and your business goals?

You'll get a chance to answer these questions in the flow-writing prompts section coming soon. This exercise will lead to *your why*.

As an example, and to be transparent and practice what I preach, here is *my why* for writing this book.

1. My book's readers feel empowered with practical tools to overcome their inner obstacles and foundational steps for enjoying the process of writing an engaging and magnetic book that helps them achieve their goals. They are excited about the accomplishment and joy they'll feel by answering the call to write their book and be of service to their readers.
2. My readers are inspired and ready to commit to getting their books into the world. They have discovered how

to move forward with a plan of action and have lined up the accountability and support they need for finishing their book.
3. My book has helped me reach a broader audience of soulful leaders looking for support to birth their books into the world, serving my business's mission of elevating conscious voices and impacting the greater good.

Notice how I answered the questions as if all this had come true already? This is a powerful way to set an intention and help manifest your desired outcome.

### FLOW-WRITING PROMPTS

Set your timer for ten minutes and answer the three questions below. Let your Inner Editor off the hook initially and write without stopping, letting your answers to the following questions pour onto the page without worrying about whether they're good writing or not. Write everything down that comes to mind.

- What is the outcome I wish for my book's readers?
- What action(s) do I want them to take after reading my book?
- How do I envision my book supporting me and my business goals?

Once you have a rough draft of your answers, take some time to edit them so they are succinct and stated in the present tense, as if they've already happened, like in my example above. Knowing these answers (*your why*) will help guide the content of your book. If you don't start with a clear vision and outcome in mind, your inner resistance will find all kinds of ways to distract you from completing your book.

To dig deeper and find even more clarity about your book, here's a free guided visualization practice with a video lesson and prompts to support you in better understanding the book that's calling you and the reader who is waiting for you to write it: www.ModernWisdomPress.com/jumpstart-your-book-journey.

## 10

# Know Your Reader

*One of the deepest longings of the human soul is to be seen.*
**JOHN O'DONOHUE**

I'LL LET YOU IN on a little secret to energetically connecting with your book's readers . . .

Write to just one reader, singular. Not readers, plural.

Even though your book may appeal to everyone, when you write it to everyone, you'll connect with no one.

Let me clarify: Although your book will undoubtedly have many readers, when you narrow your writing to address just one Ideal Reader, *all* of your readers will feel seen by you and begin to trust you as their guide.

When your Ideal Reader is the North Star of your writing journey, you are extending your hand (aka energy) to them as you would a dear friend or client, and it's palpable. Think of a book that you've read where you felt like the author was speaking directly to you. How did you feel? This kind of personal, intimate writing makes for the most memorable transformational books.

## MAGNETIZE YOUR READERS

To be able to connect with your readers through engaging writing, you must know them well. Your Ideal Reader should be someone you would enjoy spending time with, and someone with a certain challenge or problem that you're inspired to help them solve with the knowledge you plan to share in your book.

In many cases (mine included), your book's Ideal Reader may be a younger version of yourself. Many of our authors say they're inspired to write the book they wish had existed when they were facing a certain problem or challenge in their lives. That's what's calling them to write their book: to share the solution they finally figured out.

Refer to the previous chapter and remember *your why*. Understanding your goals for your book, for yourself, and for your readers can help you determine *your* Ideal Reader. Maybe it's a client. Maybe it's a colleague. Maybe it's a fictitious character. Let this person be the one who inspires you forward as you envision your book in their hands, making the impact you want to make in their life.

When I'm coaching my clients on *how* to narrow their focus to just one reader, I typically get a lot of pushback. And I get it! We think that by narrowing our focus to one type of reader with one type of problem, we'll be limiting our reach and who we can serve. And that's a myth I love to bust.

Think of it like this: When you're writing to a broad group of people (let's say women ages forty to sixty-five), your writing and voice (and therefore energy) will feel impersonal, and readers won't feel connected to you or engaged in your writing.

Our client James is a brilliant healer who developed a unique healing modality that has helped thousands of people. With thirty years of clinical experience and countless loyal clients who love his work, he came to us to write a book that would carry on his legacy and expand his reach to other practitioners who can train in his methodology and share the work with even more people.

After his first writing assignment was in, he saw he had a tendency to be overly philosophical or theoretical. This is an understandable style of writing for someone with such subject-matter expertise. Yet it felt like a firehose of information that would likely overwhelm his readers. On his next assignment, after he chose to identify one Ideal Reader and write to him as if he was sitting across from him in his office, his writing tone became more conversational and connective. James found a way to share his philosophies and theories through his own storytelling, helping his readers feel seen, stay engaged, and become excited to learn more.

When you have a particular person in mind as you write, your writing becomes much more compassionate, energetically engaging, and magnetic. Reading the book *Letters to a Young Poet* by Rainer Maria Rilke, we feel an immediate intimate connection to his writing because he's writing a letter to one person, yet this book has appealed to millions of people he wasn't writing to. (Rilke 1993) When you approach your book this way, too—like a personal letter to your reader—you open your heart with your writing, and your readers will feel that energetically.

Your writing (and energy) then becomes palpable to readers who may not be your exact Ideal Reader, yet who now see how you can help them, too. Narrowing your niche and knowing exactly who you're writing to becomes a happy paradox that

> **BOOK BIRTHING TIP**
>
> **WRITE WITH INTENTION**
>
> Light a candle before you sit down to write. Practice conscious breathing to come into the present moment. Determine where you are on the Writer Frequency Scale, and do what needs to be done to raise your energy. Call in your guides, your inner wisdom, and welcome your Inner Author. Imagine you are in a heart-to-heart conversation with your Ideal Reader, and write from there.

energizes your words. This is what makes *you* more magnetic to a broader audience.

## MEET YOUR READERS WHERE THEY ARE

As a conscious and soulful leader, you likely have holistic solutions to problems that readers may not be aware of yet. Your job as an author is to enlighten your readers with new solutions. But first, you must meet them where they are to build their trust and their desire to keep reading. Once they feel seen and understood by you, you are in the perfect position to share the solution you know they need, in *your* words.

When you write in a style that is more conversational, your readers will instantly find you relatable and are more likely to understand how your insight can help them with their unique struggle or situation.

Heartfelt, connective writing is what makes us human, real, and approachable. Have you ever read a blog or social media post and noticed that there's a lack of personality or feeling to it? Maybe the tone suddenly shifts, and it feels flat and lacks "energy" behind the words? It's a pretty good guess that it's not authentic writing from a real human (hello, AI). We all want to feel that the author of a book (or blog post) is relatable and real, reaching out to meet us through their words.

My client Lisa is an executive coach working with C-suite leaders. She was struggling with her first draft before she came to us. She felt that her writing didn't convey her confidence the same way her speaking did. She was a confident speaker and a top coach in the executive field, with stellar client testimonials.

When she dug into the exercise of identifying her Ideal Reader, she instantly thought of her favorite client, Robert, who was a CEO of a Fortune 500 company. He'd trusted her guidance as he was growing his team, and she'd seen him in his most vulnerable, burned-out moments. She knew how to meet him in his struggle and offer a solution to his most challenging problems. He became her Ideal Reader, and she taped a photo of him near her computer screen.

When Lisa sat down to write her chapters, she imagined she was sitting across from him in his thirtieth-floor corner office, having a heart-to-heart conversation. She used this vision to break through the disconnected writing style of the previous draft and instead write to him from her heart, with empathy and compassion. Her writing instantly became magnetic to the many other "Roberts" out there who needed just the kind of support Lisa had to offer.

It helps to engage your Ideal Reader by using the exact words they use to describe the challenges they are facing. Though this language may not be the way you'd describe such challenges with the current knowledge and expertise you now have, remember that your Ideal Reader may not have access to the same information as you do . . . yet.

As an example, Robert may think his main challenge is a "people problem" due to underperforming teams. But from Lisa's viewpoint, she can see that his overwhelm about quarterly performance reports is rooted in the leadership team's communication issues and burnout, which is trickling down to the teams below.

Remember how our energy can bring others up or down? As leaders, our energy awareness is a powerful tool for improving personal performance as well as that of our teams. Robert can't see that holistic viewpoint yet, but Lisa knows her book and solution will help him, so to initially engage him, she must speak/write to him in the words he's using to describe the issue, naming his concerns about his "people problem" and underperforming teams. This is especially important in the first chapter and when marketing your book, because when you speak the same language as your readers, they'll think, *This author gets me* and feel excited to buy it.

Many of our authors at MWP have attracted new clients and audiences because they chose to write to one Ideal Reader. Their readers intimately connected with their writing, so they have been able to fill up workshops, create online programs, sell digital courses, and book high-paid speaking opportunities. In many cases, they designed brand-new offerings using the framework they developed for their book.

When you write to just one Ideal Reader, describing their problem in their choice of words, you energetically engage them and magnetically attract those who need your services.

Because you've made it this far in the book, my hope is that you felt seen in Chapter 1 thinking *This author gets me!* Or perhaps you were drawn in by the book's title. You may or may not have been aware of the energetics behind flow and how you'd be guided to work with your own internal energy system, embracing the inner journey of writing your book.

I hope you now trust me as a guide who can help you bust through your obstacles—both internal and external—to achieve your dream of becoming a published book author. My desire is that these tools will help you awaken into flow and give you the clarity you need to knock out the first draft of your manuscript—and be on your way to reaping the benefits of being a published author.

## FLOW-WRITING PROMPTS

Set your timer for 15 minutes and answer the questions below. Let your intuition be your guide. Write without stopping, letting your answers flow onto the page. Write everything down that comes to mind. (See Thank You & Additional Resources for a downloadable exercise to gain even more clarity about your book's Ideal Reader.)

- Who is my book's target audience?
- Who is one person from my audience I think will most benefit from my book? *This might be a potential client, a colleague, or even a younger version of yourself.*
- What challenges are they facing without having my book?
- In *their* words, how would they describe their most pressing challenge and their perceived solution?

# 11

# Falling Out of Flow

*The secret of life is . . . to fall seven times and get up eight times.*
**PAULO COELHO**

**SOMETIMES, DEAR READER, WE** get bumped out of the flow.

That's human nature. We fall down. And we pick ourselves up, both literally and figuratively. Sometimes our minds and bodies need downtime. Time out of our busyness. Time out of doing, doing, doing.

Resting and simply being can be the indirect path back into the flow, where *doing* becomes effortless again.

I am writing this after slipping down the stairs in socks today. Ouch! My poor sacrum took the hit. I was planning to knock out a chapter, but my body and brain feel a bit scrambled. I'm physically okay, but I will take the fall as a sign to rest today. And as a metaphor for this chapter!

My ego wants to push through and try to knock out a chapter—"efforting" is quite natural for us recovering perfectionists. But I know from experience that not pushing and offering myself some kindness always pays off. Giving myself space to breathe, take a bath, or perhaps nap if I feel tired is often the best medicine. Moving around some things in my calendar and bumping my deadline a few days down the line is an act of self-love.

Hopefully, you will feel permission to be human, too—to accept the ups and downs of life, of writing a book, of stepping out of your comfort zone to create something new. Let yourself off the hook if you find that you're criticizing yourself and breathing down your own neck to keep on keeping on. Maybe what you really need is rest.

So many of us high achievers overlook the important need to nourish and refuel ourselves. We work hard to achieve our goal, then check off the box of our great feat and immediately plow forward on to the next thing on the list. This is the recipe for burnout. And it's rampant.

When I experienced burnout, I was thankfully far enough along on my personal awareness journey to see that my need to be productive and accomplished was rooted in a false childhood belief that my parents only loved me when I accomplished things. This was the natural outcome of being praised and rewarded for my accomplishments and scolded when I didn't meet the desires or goals of the adults in my life. My parents were doing the best they could with the tools they had, of course.

Most of us on a path of personal growth will have to reckon with our childhood perceptions of our worthiness, lovability, and safety if we want to get to the root and let go of our subconscious fears and limiting beliefs.

## YOU ARE ENOUGH

Many of us carry the unconscious belief that we're not lovable or "enough" unless we can prove it (and often, we find we never can). We compensate by producing, pleasing, perfecting, or performing out of a deep yearning to receive love and acceptance. Resting and prioritizing our own needs can feel risky when we're wired this way! Yet when we recognize the root of our subconscious fears and allow them to be seen and heard by our wise adult self, we lessen fear's grip on us.

Have you ever paused to reflect on all you've already accomplished and manifested in your life? Do you intentionally take time to recognize and celebrate all the little milestones and accomplishments you achieve every day?

When I first became a self-supporting adult, I used to fall asleep at night thinking about everything I had not achieved that day and planning how to catch up the next day. No wonder I ended up burned-out! My darling partner gently introduced me to his daily review practice, where at the end of the day, he spends a few moments reviewing and recognizing all he did accomplish that day and all the things that went right. Our brains have a natural negativity bias (thank you, nervous system, for trying to keep me safe!) and we have to consciously work to rewire those pathways to change our thoughts and change our reality.

## CELEBRATE YOUR ACHIEVEMENTS

Taking a break to refuel on the way to our destination and appreciating the milestones along the way can both be wonderful ways to reenergize ourselves. Just like climbing a mountain with the goal of reaching the peak for the epic views, when we write our chapters, it serves us so very well

> **BOOK BIRTHING TIP**
>
> **CELEBRATE YOURSELF**
>
> Milestones matter. Every chapter finished is worthy of celebrating. Blowing through milestones without soaking up your accomplishments leads to burnout. Rewards are nourishing fuel to sustain your momentum. Take a long, luxurious bath. Enjoy a meal out at your favorite restaurant. Book a massage.

to pause, breathe, hydrate, and refuel along the journey of finishing our book.

At MWP, each time one of our authors finishes a chapter, they share the news with the team, and we acknowledge and celebrate the accomplishment together. External accountability and acknowledgment are powerful motivators. I encourage our authors to let us know how they plan to celebrate their milestones. Sometimes, it's a splurge like a massage, and other times, it's a toast at the dinner table with their family. Be sure to plan little rewards for yourself each step of the way.

When you recognize your accomplishments—word by word and chapter by chapter—and pause to celebrate yourself for reaching a goal, no matter how small, you build confidence and energy to keep trekking onward toward your ultimate destination.

Trust the process. Enjoy the journey. Celebrate the milestones. When you prioritize self-care, it will benefit your energy and the book you're writing. How can it not?

### DISCERN THE VOICE OF YOUR SOUL

Like most who embark upon birthing a new creation into the world, you will face obstacles, doubt yourself, and perhaps want to give up. How easy it can be to blame outside circumstances. "Life just got hectic; it turns out now is not the time."

Learning to discern the voice of fear from the voice of the soul matters. Our minds can trick us into thinking that our intuition is telling us not to write our book. "It's just not time." It's important that we find a way to the truth.

Here's a simple test to gauge which voice you're hearing when thoughts pop up about your book: Do you feel contracted and small when you think or say it? Or do you feel expansive and free? Contracted and small is the voice of fear; expansive and free is the voice of the soul.

Having a greater awareness of your inner limiting thoughts and beliefs helps you discern the internal voice of fear from the voice of your soul. This understanding illuminates the way out of that catch-all excuse of writer's block. If you're stalling as a blank page stares you down, it may be your inner anxieties rearing their pretty little heads again. Welcome them as they share their worries.

*Will I be judged? What if no one cares?*

Perhaps your internal response sounds like *It's okay, fear, I get that you're feeling that way. It's understandable.*

And call on the expansive voice of your soul to soothe your worries away . . .

*You've created new things before, and you not only survived, you thrived! Isn't this offering to the world greater than your fear of judgment or disinterest? What will you gain by keeping it to yourself?*

## FIND ACCOUNTABILITY

Outside accountability can keep you out of confusion and moving down the path. Get a writing partner, a book coach, or an accountability buddy to make sure you stay on track with your intentions and goals. Support fosters sustainability.

There is nothing more empowering and encouraging than hearing someone say, "I believe in you. I see your strength. I trust in your ability to do this."

Encouragement helps us over thresholds we might otherwise never cross. Ultimately, we must believe in ourselves, but having external reinforcement can keep us afloat and moving forward. I have achieved some of my biggest accomplishments in life with the support of great coaches, teachers, midwives, healers, and loved ones, all of whom had my back and my best interests at heart. Having someone in your corner cheering you on toward your mission and goals is priceless.

## YOUR SPACE MATTERS

Some of us need a clutter-free space to get into flow. Others need the inspiration of nature or a creative environment. Whatever sparks your creative fire, bring those elements into your writing space. Create a safe place where distractions are minimal and you can focus. Whenever possible, make it an inspiring and cozy environment that liberates your Inner Author!

Here's how this has looked for me writing this book . . .

I wrote most of the chapters during winter, sitting at my desk in my home office in the mountains of Colorado. There, I have a view of the forest outside of my window, and beneath that, a beautiful altar with images that inspire me. I pour a cup of something warm and delicious, and I have a cozy wrap around my shoulders and warm, fuzzy socks on my feet. I sit down, light a candle, and

> **BOOK BIRTHING TIP**
> **SET THE SCENE**
> Create an inviting atmosphere for your Inner Author to come out to play. What sensory elements can you incorporate into your writing space to invoke a childlike sense of wonder, curiosity, and joy?

follow my breath to get present. I check in with my energy using the Writer Frequency Scale from Chapter 8. If I'm above a five on the scale, I get at it. If I'm not, I get up. I do some qigong, or I dance to an uplifting song.

As I write this chapter, however, I'm not at home. I'm out of state visiting my mother in Arkansas. I'm sitting in her home office, and my laptop is wobbling on stacks of file folders and notebooks that I'm here to help her organize!

I realize I'm not feeling that grounded or inspired, but my editor wants this manuscript tomorrow, so I must write! I just popped in my earbuds and "Sweet Dreams (Are Made of This)" by the Eurythmics is playing, leftover from an '80s playlist I had on when some friends stopped by the other night. Turns out it's the perfect song to dance to, bringing my energy up the scale from a four to a seven and helping me realize that this writing environment isn't working. I move to the glass dining table, with the room's large windows overlooking her backyard, where spring is in full bloom—the flowers and trees are budding, and red cardinals flit around her bird feeders, accompanied by a fat-faced chipmunk munching on birdseed.

I put on a new playlist I discovered while writing this book called Solfeggio Healing Frequencies. (Spotify) Each specific solfeggio tone consists of an energetic frequency, measured in hertz, that is known to help with a particular area of your well-being. This playlist was designed to help balance the chakras, and while I can't scientifically confirm that's what is happening, the music is the perfect background to help my mind focus and my words flow. So I've used it consistently while I have written these chapters. You can check out more solfeggio frequencies music on your favorite music app. If you like some background noise, choose whatever music inspires you and helps you to focus. Or maybe you prefer to write in silence. Whatever works for you!

## REBOOT YOUR ENERGY

Next time you feel stuck, remember the first step to getting back into flow: pause and breathe. *Follow the breath* for several minutes.

As your thinking naturally slows, begin to notice the thoughts in your mind. Visualize each thought floating in front of you inside of a bubble. Imagine yourself popping each bubble, one by one—and with it, the thought disappearing, too.

See what's present for you now as you dive into this next set of flow-writing prompts.

---

## FLOW-WRITING PROMPTS

Remember, let your words tumble out of you! No editing or worrying about "good" writing. Be completely honest with yourself. This writing is for your eyes only, though the more transparent you are with those you trust, the more support you can receive when you need it most.

- Where am I stuck, and which tools can help me move forward right now?
- Do I need an accountability partner or coach? Who do I trust to support me through this?
- What milestones have I achieved that I can celebrate now?
- What milestones lie ahead, and what kinds of rewards can I give to myself for achieving them?

## 12

# Coming Back Into Flow

*I do not at all understand the mystery of grace—only that it meets us where we are but does not leave us where it found us.*
**ANNE LAMOTT**

**WRITING A BOOK THAT** will inspire and help others transform is a rewarding and sometimes very challenging journey. You can bet you will be tested along the way.

I've lost count of the times I have felt like a fraud writing this book! I've done exactly what my book-coaching clients drive me nuts doing: I've second-guessed myself, rethought and reorganized my chapters, and missed my writing deadlines for other "more important things."

Writing this book has not been all joy or all flow. There have been times when I didn't feel clear or inspired, and times I wondered why the heck I decided to write a book about writing a book with flow! Classic impostor syndrome.

But this is how life works. It just can't be all joy and flow. There are highs and lows, ups and downs, and we must learn how to navigate the ebb and flow of our writing, too. Which is why we need tools to pick ourselves up when we've fallen out of flow.

From everything I've learned about getting unstuck (in many areas of my life), I've found the answer lies in cultivating more self-trust.

Writing is an inner experience. We spend a lot of time alone with our thoughts and can therefore often get hung up in our heads. We overthink, swim in self-doubt, pick things apart with our perfectionism, or write in circles—all attributed to the popular excuse of writer's block.

Self-trust stops all of that. It starts when we slow down our busy minds and seek out the voice of our intuition or soul. By listening to and trusting the inner voice that feels expansive and aligned with our bigger purpose, we access our inner wisdom. We can trust its guidance, no matter the risks we must take to follow it.

We each have an important choice to make as we embark upon writing a book. We can choose to stay stuck in our limiting beliefs or fears, or we can reach beyond ourselves for something bigger to guide us, trusting in whatever is calling us to write *through* us. This will help us get out of our own way and be of service to our readers.

When you're willing to embrace the inner journey of transformation as you write, something magical happens: You become transformed by your book. You birth a stronger, wiser version of yourself.

So pull out your commitment statement, and if you haven't signed it already, here's your chance. Put it on your desk or somewhere you'll see it often to remind you of *your why*. Let this commitment to yourself and your future readers keep you on the path, moving toward the finish line of becoming a published book author.

When you're ready to write, refer to the Writer Frequency Scale in Chapter 8 to assess and elevate your energy, ensuring your words connect and resonate with your Ideal Reader.

And when you're unsure, confused, or bumped out of flow, use the FLOW Method to balance your intellect with your intuition and your mind with your heart through the guided chakra breathing practices and flow-writing prompts. These practices have helped me and the many authors I've coached get back into flow and finish their books.

> BOOK BIRTHING TIP
>
> **SHARE YOUR SUCCESS**
>
> When you meet a deadline or finish a chapter, share the good news! Posting about your book as you write it can help build excitement, future book sales, and momentum toward your ultimate goals.

> Follow the breath.
> Let go of fear.
> Own your inner wisdom.
> Write from the heart.

If your thoughts are spiraling in a negative way and you've got a case of stinkin' thinkin', come back to *your why*. Come back to your inner wisdom. Come back to your readers who are waiting for your book. And use the positive affirmations from Chapter 7 when you need a quick prop to boost your confidence and get back into flow.

If you're truly committed to your calling, you must be willing to examine the obstacles in your way and uncover the subconscious fears and patterns at their root. When you see that the inner journey of gestating and birthing your book is just as crucial as the outer one, you'll embark upon a powerful opportunity for transformation—both for yourself and for your readers.

We all have the capacity to awaken into flow and create what our souls are calling us to create. How we choose to express our creative energy is unique to each of us. Remember that it doesn't matter how many books have been written about your topic. Your unique lens of experience, your unique voice, and your unique way of expressing yourself will make your book stand apart from others. Your words can express your unique energetic signature, attracting those who are meant to find you.

Your soul's expression is an important thread of the tapestry of life. The ripple effect of your commitment and effort to birth your book into the world is mysteriously infinite. Your energetic flow is part of the Divine dance of this Universe. Your voice matters. You are worthy of shining. When you align your energy to embrace your creative callings and take action to bring them into reality, you step into the energy of flow and are forever transformed.

So, dear reader, what are you waiting for?

---

**FLOW-WRITING PROMPT**

Let me leave you with one final flow-writing prompt. Set your timer for thirty minutes and write a letter to your Ideal Reader on the topic of "Why I Wrote This Book."

Tell your reader about your calling, *your why*, and the inspiration you feel to guide and serve them. Visualize your book in your reader's hands and the feeling you have of finally accomplishing this dream. Write from your heart, without stopping, without editing, without needing it to be "good" writing. Just flow.

Let this final flow-writing experience become your manifesto to guide you forward on your book-writing journey.

And know that I am here, cheering you on!

# References

Cameron, Julia. *The Artist's Way*. 2016. TarcherPerigee.

Cristol, Hope, Kristin Mitchell, and Angela McPhillips. "Dopamine: What It Is & What It Does." Medically reviewed on July 9, 2024 by Jabeen Begum. WebMD.com. https://www.webmd.com/mental-health/what-is-dopamine.

Csikszentmihalyi, Mihaly. *Flow: The Psychology of Optimal Experience*. 2008. Harper Perennial Modern Classics.

Dale, Cyndi. *The Subtle Body: An Encyclopedia of Your Energetic Anatomy*. 2009. Sounds True.

Emoto, Masaru. "Science of Water." Masaru-Emoto.net. https://masaru-emoto.net/en/science-of-messages-from-water/.

Epstein, Joseph. "Think You Have a Book in You? Think Again." New York Times. September 28, 2002. https://www.nytimes.com/2002/09/28/opinion/think-you-have-a-book-in-you-think-again.html.

Goswami, Amit. "The Idealistic Interpretation of Quantum Mechanics." 1989. Physics Essays.

Halliday, D., R. Resnick, & J. Walker. *Fundamentals of Physics* (10th ed.). 2014. Wiley.

HeartMath Institute. *Science of the Heart: Exploring the Role of the Heart in Human Performance.* E-book; Chapter 6. HeartMath.org. https://www.heartmath.org/research/science-of-the-heart/energetic-communication/.

Rilke, Rainer Maria. *Letters to a Young Poet.* 1993. W. W. Norton & Company.

McCraty, Rollin. "The Energetic Heart: Bioelectromagnetic Communication Within and Between People." 2004. https://www.heartmath.org/research/research-library/energetics/energetic-heart-bioelectromagnetic-communication-within-and-between-people/.

Mitchell, Kristin, and Nechama F. Sammet Moring. "The 7 Chakras for Healing and Energy." December 1, 2023. WebMD.com. https://www.webmd.com/balance/what-are-chakras.

Rumi, Jalaluddin. "The Guest House." From *Rumi: Selected Poems.* Translated by Coleman Barks. 2004. Penguin Books.

Santos, Andrea. "So'ham. I Am That." August 10, 2020 (update from pub July 24). Yogapedia.com. https://www.yogapedia.com/2/7214/meditation/mantra/soham-i-am-that.

Spotify. Chakra Healing Frequencies: Solfeggio Chakras. Playlist. https://open.spotify.com/playlist/71A8ZTnUbzUNXPJwBTN7jf.

Van der Linden, Dimitri, Mattie Tops, and Arnold B. Bakker. "The Neuroscience of the Flow State." April 14, 2021. Frontiers in Psychology. FrontiersIn.org. https://www.frontiersin.org/journals/psychology/articles/10.3389/fpsyg.2021.645498/full.

# About the Author

**CATHERINE S. GREGORY** is a transformational book coach and cofounder of Modern Wisdom Press. She is also a certified meditation instructor and intuitive healer trained in energy medicine and other holistic healing modalities from across the globe. As an award-winning author and editor with a BA in Journalism, she has more than twenty-five years in the publishing industry.

Catherine brings her 15 years of experience in energy healing and transformational coaching to the creative process of the book-birthing journey. She is the creator of the FLOW Method and is passionate about supporting others on the inner journey of becoming a transformational book author. Catherine blends her hybrid skill set into a potent program that empowers soulful leaders to write and publish books that showcase their expertise while making a positive impact.

A mystic, nature lover, and enthusiastic student of life, Catherine lives in the San Luis Valley of southern Colorado with her partner in life and business, Nathan Joblin. They are the cofounders of Modern Wisdom Press and stewards of several magical acres of high-alpine desert fed by a seasonal creek. They are also the proud parents of a blended family of four adult children and two fur babies.

# Acknowledgments

**THIS BOOK** could not exist without the amazing souls who have trusted me to support them in writing and publishing their books. Thank you, thank you to each brilliant author of Modern Wisdom Press. What a gift! I am personally transformed by every author and manuscript that blesses my path. Truly. Thank you for trusting me and for being willing to dive deep into the inner journey of writing your books. I am humbled and honored to grow with you and know your transformational books are changing countless lives and rippling positive energy into the world!

I want to give an extra dose of gratitude to Dr. Jamie Shapiro, author of *Brilliant: Be the Leader Who Shines Brightly Without Burning Out,* for your generosity and support over the years since you wrote your first book. We are all blessed by the incredible leaders you've sent our way to write their books and for the impact your important work is making in the world.

To the expert Modern Wisdom Press team of editors, designers, and publishing sages (especially Melinda, M.C., Karen S., Felicia, Erika, Dave, Julie, Minhaj, and Melissa), whose talents and heartful service make book dreams come true. A special bow to Karen Polaski, the talented designer who brought the vision for this book's cover and interior design to life. To all my friends and colleagues who offered endorsements and book launch team support. And to the lovely Ariel Levy-Mayer, who reined us in to consistently create and expand our marketing outreach and online presence—no small feat.

To all the heart-led teachers and support on my path, especially my coach Steve Havill, for seeing my gifts of midwifery magic before I even did! And to Suzanne Forester, Nicteha Cohen, and Josephine Hart, for sharing your wisdom and generously guiding me back to my body and wholeness during the months of gestating and birthing this book. To my parents Watt and Susan, for your lifelong love, support, and encouragement to follow my dreams! And to Ella and Silas, for cheering me on and continually inspiring me with your creative, courageous hearts.

To my spiritual support team here and beyond, for the inspiration to live from my heart day by day and use my Divine gifts to serve in my unique way. To my muse—the wild mountains, hot springs, desert dunes, and big magical skies of the San Luis Valley. I'm so grateful to be home again.

And last but most certainly not least, thanks to my true partner in life and business Nathan Joblin. Thank you for all you do to support our authors and bring their life-changing books into the world. You make co-leadership fun! I am blessed to dance this dance with you. My deepest gratitude for your love, support, and commitment to grow together in partnership for the highest good of all.

May this book be of benefit to all who read it.

# Thank You & Additional Resources

**DEAR READER,**

If you've read through this book and arrived here, I want to thank you. Thank you for reading my book, and really, thank you for being you—a soulful leader who wants to write a book that positively changes lives!

I hope that you're feeling empowered with new inspiration, insight, and tools to move forward on your journey of writing your transformational book.

To further support your book-writing adventure, I have a gift for you. Please visit www.ModernWisdomPress.com/bookgift to access these three free resources:

1. A downloadable **Writer Frequency Scale** to keep handy when you're ready to write.
2. A downloadable **Commitment Statement** to sign and keep you on the path.
3. An **Ideal Reader Exercise** to help you get clarity about who you're writing to.

**For more tips and guidance** to help get your transformational book into the world, subscribe to the Modern Wisdom Press monthly newsletter at www.ModernWisdomPress.com/subscribe.

**And if you're ready for personalized accountability and support** in becoming a published book author, let's talk! Tell us more at www.ModernWisdomPress.com/letstalk and we'll be in touch to see how we can best support you.

Finally, for more on mindfulness, presence, consciousness, and creative energy, here are some of my favorite books:

*The Power of Now* by Eckhart Tolle
*Living Beautifully: with Uncertainty and Change* by Pema Chödrön
*Breathe, You Are Alive* by Thich Nhat Hahn
*The Untethered Soul* by Michael Singer
*Polishing the Mirror* by Ram Dass
*The Artist's Way* by Julia Cameron
*Bird by Bird* by Anne Lamott
*The Creative Act: A Way of Being* by Rick Rubin

To your inner wisdom,
Catherine

# About Modern Wisdom Press

**FOUNDED BY** Catherine Gregory and Nathan Joblin in 2019, Modern Wisdom Press is dedicated to elevating conscious voices by empowering visionary leaders and subject-matter experts to find clarity, ease, and joy in writing and publishing their transformational nonfiction books.

Our values and core principles are rooted in conscious leadership, which begins with self-awareness and intentionality, awakening more fulfillment and purpose in your life and those you lead. We support aspiring authors who are here to make a positive impact, with the ripple effect benefiting not only their readers, but also their families, communities, and beyond.

www.ingramcontent.com/pod-product-compliance
Lightning Source LLC
Chambersburg PA
CBHW030443090526
44586CB00044B/624